# FIRST STEPS IN PRAYER

# FIRST STEPS
# IN PRAYER

*Cardinal*
*Jean-Marie Lustiger*

*Translated by Rebecca Howell Balinski*

**Doubleday**
NEW YORK
1987

Library of Congress Cataloging-in-Publication Data
Lustiger, Jean-Marie, 1926–
  First steps in prayer.
  Translation of: Premiers pas dans la prière.
  1. Prayer. I. Title.
BV210.2.L8713  1987     248.3′2     87–6730
ISBN 0-385-24188-7

Originally published in French under the title *Premiers Pas Dans La Prière*, 1986, Nouvelle Cité, Paris, Copyright © 1986 Nouvelle Cité. English Translation Copyright © 1987 by Doubleday & Company, Inc.

Biblical quotations are taken from *The New Oxford Annotated Bible, an Ecumenical Study Bible* (Revised Standard Version), Oxford University Press, New York, 1977.

# CONTENTS

# FOREWORD

This book brings together sixteen talks on prayer given by the Archbishop of Paris on Radio Notre-Dame from August 29 to November 28, 1984. Summaries or extracts of these talks were published weekly in the diocesan bulletin, *Paris Notre-Dame*.

The response to both the radio talks and their "chosen bits" which were printed has led the cardinal to revise and edit the original texts in order to reach as broad an audience as possible. There is no point in looking here for an exhaustive treatise on spirituality or even, strictly speaking, for a manual on prayer. But in his role as father, the Archbishop of Paris simply and almost spontaneously guides the reader along the first steps of spiritual progress, so that he or she can begin, or begin again, to follow in the steps of Christ.

This initiation to prayer goes well beyond practical advice and encouragement, and presents a way of living as well as an entire catechesis: because a person prays the way he believes, and he lives the way he prays.

*FIRST STEPS IN PRAYER*

# FIRST STEP

*Every Day*

We must pray every day. I repeat, every day. Why? Because we are made that way.

We are beings shaped by God from the dust of our earth. Think, for example, of the problems that arise for the human psyche when a person begins to tear himself away from his earthly environment by space flights and moon landings. Regardless of his environment, a person has to keep to his innate biological rhythm, a rhythm that connects him with the earth and all living creatures on it. The first chapter of Genesis reminds us: there are days and nights, evenings and mornings.

Our lives take place in time. Freedom, our most beautiful and highest faculty, allied with our intelligence and our capacities for willing and loving, the fine point of our being which turns toward God, is, nevertheless, exercised in our lifetimes. It is the freedom given to creatures of flesh and blood who are called from day to day to live from the present moment in the eternity of God.

Thus, when a person commits his life to God, he must recommit it each day. You all know the request in the Lord's Prayer: "Give us this day our daily bread." No matter how the phrase is interpreted, the emphasis remains on "this day." Jesus, just as the prophets and men of God before him, asks us to measure the duration of our existence from day to day, by the new day that succeeds the one just finishing, from the beginning to the end of our lives. It is within our days that our lives and our freedom are inscribed.

To offer our lives to God each day means accepting each day as a gift from God, and giving it back to him in a prayer of thanksgiving, blessing, praise, and supplication. In short, we are to speak to God just as a son speaks to a father who he knows loves him; or according to Ignatius of Loyola, "as a friend speaks to a friend" *(Spiritual Exercises,* No. 54).

So much for the spirit in which man must pray every day. What kind of prayer should it be? To answer, I quote some words that Jesus spoke in the Sermon on the Mount: "When you pray, go into your room and shut the door and pray to your Father who is in secret" (Matthew 6:6). Of course, Jesus is speaking directly to people who live in villages and, no doubt, still have the physical possibility of withdrawing in such a way. But his admonition applies to all men, in all times.

Each disciple of Christ must seek out that secret place, a place where God can reveal to him the paternal love he has for his children, and where the disciple, in complete honesty, can be liberated from all exterior constraints and, in particular, stripped of all masks. Hidden from human eyes, freed from the judgment of others and "what people will say," he is no longer required to keep up a front. In his secret retreat, he can present himself before God alone.

Whoever you are, whatever the conditions of your life, even if you are in a hospital room, or a cramped apartment, or traveling by subway, even if you are in the middle of a pressing crowd, you have the possibility

of finding that "interior room" where you can go and
close the door. That's not easy, you will say. I know, and
it does depend somewhat on temperaments. I pray better in the mountains, where there are no human voices,
only the birds' songs. But I assure you that you can pray
in the subway, in a workshop or factory, and even in an
office, a hospital, or barracks. And when there is no
other way, you can simply pull the bedcovers over your
head and pray before you go to sleep.

It is always practicable to find a way of creating
that interior solitude where the freedom and authenticity of our dialogue with God are proven by the con-
stancy of our decision to pray.

Pray every day. Pray in secret. I will add something
else: pray at least in the morning and in the evening.
Those of you who are older are probably smiling because the mention of praying in the morning and evening brings back memories! What, after all, is the special significance of praying at these particular times of
day?

At the end of the day, I get ready to fall asleep and
give myself up to the night. By abandoning myself to
sleep, I prepare for the rest which is essential for my
body, my mind, my psyche, the rest which will restore
my strength. For many of us, getting to sleep often
involves a not always successful struggle with insomnia
or tensions arising from our stressful lives. Whatever
the difficulties of the moment, the Christian tradition
invites each of us to take the time before we fall asleep
to unite ourselves with Christ himself.

Actually, the Church teaches us the words for this
evening prayer, which are a phrase from Psalm 31 spoken by Christ just before his death: *"Father, into thy*

*hands I commit my spirit"* (Luke 23:46). By trusting, like Christ, in the sovereign liberty of God, we associate ourselves—not just at the hour when we are confronted with death, but each evening—with the abandon of Christ into the hands of his Father. Thus, falling asleep becomes an act of confidence in the goodness of God: he will release us from the tensions of the day and the harsh realities of life. To pray in the evening is to fall asleep in Christ; it is, along with Christ, to abandon ourselves to God. Not for death, but for life. We abandon to him the very breath and minds that we have received from him. Not in the spirit of giving back something that was borrowed, but rather of seeking to "inspire" and open our lives more fully to God, who is Life and who gives life. And so, that is the evening prayer: putting ourselves in God's hands.

Now for the morning prayer. When you wake up, instead of sluggishly shaking off your sleepiness and fatigue like an animal and then rushing about frantically so as not to be late, you must, before doing anything else, take a moment, however brief, to praise the coming day and your awakening to it. Your awakening is given to you as an event in the Creation of the world *and* of your life. Accept each day, then, as a brief period in your life when you can once again receive the existence that springs freely from the hand of God. Accept it as a Resurrection, a rising up with Christ.

\*   \*   \*   \*

Contemporary society tends to adopt a mechanistic attitude toward life. Because we know that an automobile, a motorcycle, a bicycle, or coffee grinder has a limited life span, that it will function for approximately so many hours and that one day it will simply wear out, we are tempted to imagine that the same is true for human beings and the world. Admittedly, the functioning of the body, and of the universe as well, when viewed on a certain level can be understood mechanically: it works, it slows down, and, eventually, it stops. It is not replaceable and it can be repaired only with great difficulty. But that is the wrong way of looking at our existence.

Each day of a human being's life is a wondrous event! An event that must be acknowledged as a gift from God, an interval of time when we are given the freedom to love him and to love our brothers, to adore him and to witness to his splendor before men who are created in the image and likeness of his beloved Son. We are being given yet another day to live with the goal of accomplishing our respective tasks, those missions entrusted to us by God, who brought us into existence and gives us life. Each day must be accepted as a bounty that God, our Creator and our Father, is making to us at this specific time. Not that we are created anew each day; we do, however, receive Creation as something new in the sense that our freedom has been returned to its state of innocence through God's forgiveness, and it has been restored to its glory by the gifts of the Holy Spirit. Each morning, when we rise from our sleep, the Holy Spirit allows us to rise with Christ, to begin our day with Christ in the freshness of the Easter dawn.

In the morning prayer, we give thanks to God for his blessings—the day, ourselves, our life and freedom; we give thanks that we can participate with Christ in the Resurrection; we give thanks that we can enter—by means of this new day dedicated to our respective activities—into the communion of men loved by God. Each day the Holy Spirit brings together into the Church of Christ all the children of God who are scattered abroad, in order that they can be associated with Christ's plan for the salvation of the world.

Yes, each gesture of human life is biologically conditioned, but it symbolizes much more than anyone is able to discern in it. Thus, when a person eats, he is not just satisfying his hunger: he can announce in advance the Eucharist of Christ.

Fellow Christians, by the grace which is given to us, we can throughout the day—and not only *"seven times a day"*—create the occasions for offerings and praise addressed to God our Father.

# SECOND STEP

## A Simple Sign

Having talked about the necessity of learning to pray every day, let us now turn to a passage that tells about the early Church's practice regarding daily prayer and the times for it. It comes from *The Apostolic Tradition*, written by Hippolyte of Rome at the beginning of the third century.

*"All the faithful, men and women, from the moment of their morning awakening, before doing anything else whatsoever, are to first wash their hands [as a sign of spiritual as well as physical purification] and pray to God; and only afterwards are they to begin their usual activities. And if there is a meeting for the instruction of Christians, they must attend. . . . On the days when there is no instruction, then each person, in his own home, is to take a holy book [the reference is to the books of the Bible] and is to read it for as long as is necessary for obtaining some profit from it.*

*If you are at home at the third hour of the day, pray and praise God; but, if you are elsewhere, pray to God in your heart, because it was at the third hour that Christ was nailed to wood.*

*In the same way, pray again at the sixth hour, because while Christ was still attached to the wood of the Cross, the day was interrupted and there was a great darkness over the land. You are to pray fervently at this hour also.*

*At the ninth hour, the period of prayer and praise is to be prolonged, following the example of the souls of the righteous who praise God who is always truthful, who remembered his saints and sent his Word to enlighten them. Because at the ninth hour Christ, pierced in his side, shed water and blood, lighting what remained of the day before evening fell.*

*Pray, also, before you go to your nightly rest.*

*Toward the middle of the night, arise, wash your hands with water and pray. If your wife is present, pray with her. If, however, she is not yet a believer, go into another room to pray, and then return to your bed.*

*Do not be slothful in prayer.*

Do you not find those words, written almost eighteen centuries ago, extraordinary? From the beginning, Christians have been keenly conscious of their obligations concerning prayer which they are to fulfill in the spiritual temple formed by the Church. You may be thinking, "Well, of course, they had plenty of time." Not at all! Man *never* has time. God *gives* it to him. Man must *take* it.

The simplest way to pray, a way that we all know, is to make the sign of the Cross. With it, according to the custom of the Western Church, we mark our body from forehead to chest, from one shoulder to the other, and, thus, trace a cross on ourselves. Hippolyte, whom I just cited, speaks also about the sign of the Cross. Let us take a moment to think about its significance.

First of all, it is a prayer of movement, a prayer of both the body and the spirit. We are not merely thinking, but are physically associating all our being with the act of prayer. Our entire existence is seized in all its dimensions by the power of God's love which is given to us.

Why, specifically, the sign of the Cross? Because it is the reminder of the distinctive mark made on us at the time of our baptism (the "signation" of our baptism, we can call it), and also of our confirmation, when the sign of the Cross is traced with chrism on the forehead of the baptized. This practice has deep biblical roots. In chapter 9, verse 4, of Ezekiel, God calls a mysterious individual and says to him, "Go through the city, through Jerusalem, and put a mark [with the letter *T*, *tav*, in Hebrew] upon the foreheads of the men who sign and groan over all the abominations that are comitted in it." The prophet explains that at the hour of Judgment, all those who have been marked on their foreheads by the sacred sign, the *tav*, will be saved by the angel of God: a reminder of Passover. And in Revelations, chapter 7, verse 3, the Apostle John describes those who will be marked on the forehead by the sign of the Lamb.

\* \* \* \*

The first lesson to be learned from this evocation of the sign made on our foreheads at baptism and confirmation is that when we make it on ourselves, we are recalling the sign that was given to us by another. We did not mark ourselves with the sign of the Cross. We received it. From whom? From the priest who baptized us, and the bishop who confirmed us, of course; but, more fundamentally, we received it from the Church and, hence, from Christ. It is the sign of Christ par excellence, the sign of the Lamb. Thus, by this simple gesture that I make on myself, I recall the communion of which I am a part, the people to whom I belong, a people made up of brothers and sisters of the Messiah, all of them marked in the same way with the paschal sign. Furthermore, by this gesture I am reunited with the innumerable host of those who share the condition of Christ since they have become the children of God, our Father.

\* \* \* \*

The sign of the Cross is, moreover, a reminder that I am "conformed" to Christ, that I am one with him who was crucified and resurrected. The earlier brief citation from Ezekiel, recalling the Exodus, led us to understand this already. And Saint John in Revelations, in referring to Christ, dead and resurrected, as the sacrificed Lamb, reveals the depth of the paschal mystery. That is why, when making the sign of the Cross on ourselves, we evoke the memory of our salvation, given to us by Christ, and we dispose ourselves to be seized by him again. We measure again the largess of God's grace, which has permitted us to die to sin with Christ who died for our sins and to begin already to partake of his life. We are reminded, too, that because of the power of the resurrected Christ with whom we are one, we have received the strength to face the struggle with death.

I remember that I am saved by Christ the Savior, and that, redeemed by him, I am associated with the mystery of the Cross and participate in the salvation of those people around me, of the entire world. When I trace the Cross of the Lord on my body, all the misery of the world reposes on me, but it is a misery that has been transfigured and transformed into deliverance and salvation. It is a mystery of the Redemption which envelops me from head to toe, in all the dimensions of my existence—past, present, and future. Future? Yes, future, because the sign of the Cross announces the victory of the Crucified, the hope of the Resurrection.

* * * *

As I make the sign of the Cross, I pronounce these words: *"In the name of the Father, and of the Son, and of the Holy Spirit,"* and with them I advance still further into the mystery of God. Although he is invisible, unknowable, and unfathomable to human beings with their weaknesses and limitations, God makes himself known. In fact, through love, he adopts us and shapes us into brothers and sisters of Christ, the eternal Son. And he fills us with the power of his Holy Spirit, who transfigures us in the here and now and gives us a foretaste of eternal life, a life of holiness: true happiness and the fulfillment of our existence.

When I sign myself with the Cross of Christ at the beginning of the day as I repeat, *"In the name of the Father, and of the Son, and of the Holy Spirit,"* I assess anew the divine vocation of man. It is divine not only because man is created in the image and likeness of God, but also because God, in sending his eternal Son to take on the human condition, makes it possible for me, a poor creature, a sinner marked by death, to enter into the divine vocation of the Son of God.

Invoking the name of the Father, the Son, and the Spirit requires us to take a step further in the faith. By these words, I enter into the mystery of God, into the unity of his Nature and the Trinity of Persons whom I

adore. By grace, it has been given to me to take part in
the actual life of God. When the mystery of God is
contemplated in this way, I am seized by it, and from
that moment I carry it within me. The sign of the Cross,
light for my life and light for the world, reveals the
Christian's task for each day: to be a witness to the
Father, the Son, and the Holy Spirit. By the gift of the
Spirit, we—along with all our human brothers whom
God has called—participate in the condition of the Son
in order to praise the Heavenly Father.

\* \* \* \*

Finally, the last dimension of the Sign of the Cross
is its spatial symbolism, its four cardinal points. We must
not forget it, because while man can be carried out of
the earth's sphere of gravity by rockets, he must, nevertheless, keep his feet solidly planted on the ground. The
Church Fathers and all of Christian tradition have em-
phasized this cosmic symbolism. It remains meaningful
for all people who are sensitive to the world around
them.

When I make this gesture on my body—from north
to south, from east to west—my poor bodily existence
and the irreplaceable treasure of its singularity, your
existence, the existence of our brothers who are also
listening—in short, the existence of each one of us—is
inscribed in the totality of the cosmos and is destined to
make those parts of the world where we are placed
brilliant with the splendor of God. By the sign of the
Cross, Christians recognize and declare their common
vocation and go forth to fulfill it.

Yes, the sign of the Cross is a simple way to pray.
You can easily grasp the richness of this Christian sign,

*"In the name of the Father, and of the Son, and of the Holy Spirit,"* especially if you happen to worship in a community that has rediscovered—and young people have helped us greatly in this way—the gesticulation of prayer. And if you are not just a brain with feet, cramped by a false modesty, ossified and paralyzed by the atheism of our society and, hence, utterly incapable of expressing with your body that you were born from On High, then you, too, may be able to discover or rediscover the gesticulation of prayer.

Personally, I delight in being able to dip my hand into a basin of holy water—beautiful, pure and fresh. It calls to mind baptismal water and the Easter Watch. Then, I can not only make the sign of the Cross "in the name of the Father, and of the Son, and of the Holy Spirit," but, by touching my head and chest with this water, I can recall the wealth of its symbolism which gives my life its grandeur: the first water of Creation over which the Spirit of God moved; the water of the Red Sea crossed by the Hebrews chosen to enter into a Covenant with God; the water of the River Jordan, on the threshold of the Promised Land; the water of baptism; the water of tears which wash away our sins; living water (cf. John 4:7–16) that God causes to well up in us, like a spring gushing forth from the Spirit.

So you see, when we get up in the morning, we can pray very simply: *"In the name of the Father, and of the Son, and of the Holy Spirit."*

# THIRD STEP

## Open Your Bible

How are we to respond to the Lord's commandment to pray every day? Earlier, I pointed out several practical as well as spiritual considerations regarding our existence, which is marked by sleeping and waking, days and nights, evenings and mornings. As one day succeeds another, we must inscribe in each of them the presence of God and our attention to him, for as long as we live. All reality that affects our bodies, our being, is a sign and demonstration of the reality of our existence. Nothing in human existence, material and bodily, is without meaning; it is through my body that I receive my existence. In my bodily condition I am capable of understanding and seeing the mission to which God calls me. In my bodily as well as my spiritual existence, I can and must praise and serve God, exercising the freedom he gives me. That is why it is important to pray every day, when we wake up and when we go to bed, with whatever aids are necessary, so that our lives can realize their potential beauty, and so that we can live them with the assurance of faith, the peace of love, and the joy of hope which dwell in the Christian heart.

*   *   *   *

Here is a good suggestion, but it does require patience and perseverance to put into practice. (I am thinking in particular of Christians who lead lives with densely packed hours, who are overloaded by outside demands and constraints—but my proposals are equally valid for anyone.) You will find it extremely fruitful to stock your memory with words that God has written in human hearts, in order to reveal his love for all people. In this way, your imagination and sensibility become saturated by these words, and eventually your lips will begin to form the words of God himself. The word *God* would not make sense if God had not revealed himself in our language.

When we try to speak with God, whom human language is incapable even of naming, we stammer and search for words. Often the words do not come at all. There is really nothing surprising about that. Being articulate sometimes means that we are at ease with a subject or with the person to whom we are speaking. Once we touch on delicate and subtle matters, however, we no longer know very well what to say, and sometimes we are simply at a total loss for words. The deepest sentiments, the most fervent convictions, the keenest admirations, or the most intense cries of horror are inexpressible in human words. We remain speechless. Those among you who have been struck dumb in the presence of another person will understand what I mean. How many times do we go away from a meeting or a conversation reproaching ourselves, "Oh, I do wish I had said this or that. Not only was I unable to find words to express all that I was thinking—even though I had prepared them beforehand—but even worse, the words which came did not express what I had in my head, in my heart."

\*　\*　\*　\*

In order to pray, we must enrich our imagination, nourish our sensibility, and find the appropriate words. How? In learning *by heart* the prayers that are a part of the language that God has given to us as a means of speaking both to him *and* to the human heart. Do you find that definition complicated? Well then, let us get straight to the point: memorize some Psalms and repeat them to yourself regularly.

Your first reaction may be, "But the Psalms are so long!" No, not necessarily. Leaf through your Bible and you will notice that there are some short ones as well, some having no more than four lines. In the beginning, just choose them according to length. You will fall on some little masterpieces! It is important, by the way, to remember that the length or brevity of a Psalm was not determined by chance. In these songs and poems which God has inspired his people to use when praying to him and praising him, there is a direct connection between their literary form, verse arrangement, and content. The short Psalms are extraordinarily forceful and beautiful expressions of a variety of spiritual attitudes: praise, supplication, and so forth. They present us with a manner of praying that gives words to our lips while giving to our hearts and our faith the nourishment necessary to endure while speaking to God.

Go ahead, then, and open your Bible to the book of Psalms. You will rediscover many phrases and verses which are familiar to you and which you know how to sing. But you will frequently be surprised to discover a Psalm in its entirety. The Liturgy of the Word, heard during the Sunday and weekday Masses, has accustomed us to read only three or four stanzas consisting of four lines, regardless of the Psalm's length.

Rather than risk distorting its full meaning, I prefer to take a complete Psalm, whether it is short or rather long, and to read it through from beginning to end, as it was conceived by the person whom God inspired to give his prayer to a people.

\* \* \* \*

So learn some Psalms by heart, keeping in mind as you do so that they are the prayers of the People of Israel and of all of God's People, the prayers of the Virgin Mary and of the Church today, as they were yesterday and will be tomorrow. But the principal point to remember is that the Psalms are the prayers of Jesus himself. Through the words of a Psalm committed to memory we enter into an immense and brilliant resonance of multiple harmonies, into the prayer of Jesus himself which inscribes itself across all time and all centuries and becomes the prayer of all the world, of the cosmos in its plenitude, to the glory of God.

The Psalms teach us how God reveals himself in the language of men and women, and how he inspires us to sing his praises. You will find everything in the Psalms, as the great mystics from Saint Bernard to Bossuet never ceased to repeat, as did the earliest monks and Church Fathers, such as Saint Ambrose, who wrote a magnificent commentary on the First Psalm:

*If anyone wishes to sum up the history of the "ancients" and wishes to follow their examples, he has all the progression of their history condensed into a single Psalm. And thanks to its terseness, he will be able to keep it in his memory. If anyone wishes to discover the strength of the Law, which is based entirely on the bond of love [because he who loves his neighbor has fulfilled the law perfectly], let him read in the Psalms about the neighborly love of a single man who, in order to repel the injury done to an entire people, exposes himself to great danger. He will learn there that the glory of love is not inferior to the triumph of bravery. . . .*

*Is there anything better than a Psalm? David rightly says, "Praise the Lord, because the Psalm is a good thing. Tender and beautiful praise to our God!" And that is true, because the Psalm is a blessing pronounced by the people, praise to God by the congregation, applause by all, word spoken by the universe, voice of the Church, melodious profession of faith, complete celebration of the hierarchy, exhilaration of freedom, exclamation of joy, quiver of enthusiasm. It calms anger, takes away our cares, comforts our sadness. It protects us from the night, it instructs us for the day. It is a shield for the fearful, a feast for the pious, a ray of tranquility, a guarantee of peace and harmony. Like a zither it combines in a single melody diverse and unequal voices. The Psalm is echoed by the dawn, and at sunset it is still reverberating.*

*Instruction and charm compete in a Psalm: we sing it for our delight, and at the same time, we learn it to edify ourselves. What riches are found when you read the Psalms! When I read "Hymn for the Beloved," I am set ablaze with the desire for divine love. In the Psalms I find brought together the grace of revelations, the prophecies of the resurrection, the treasure of promises.*

*From them, I learn to avoid sin, I unlearn the shame of doing penance for my faults.*[1]

Remember, Saint Augustine was converted to the Catholic faith by the beauty and richness of the Psalms, and from the earliest days of the Church, Christians knew the Psalter by heart.

Perhaps you think learning Psalms is archaic? Just try it. Open a Psalter, immerse yourself in it, and begin to memorize some of the gems you will find there. You will see, the experience is sublime! By repeating the Psalms by heart, we enter into the prayer of the Church. Those among you who have a little more time for morning and evening prayers can use the Psalms that the Church has collected and set aside as prayers for Christian gatherings. Priests and nuns are no longer the only ones to consecrate their lives to the duty of praying! This collection, called in earlier times a breviary, is known today as *The Liturgy of the Hours.* You will find it in most bookstores. I recommend that you buy it and use it!

\*    \*    \*    \*

Suppose you open your Bible and learn by heart and *with* heart the shortest of the Psalms that you find. Take Psalm 117, for example:

Praise the Lord, all Nations!
Extol him, all peoples!
For great is his steadfast love

[1] cf. *Liturgy of the Hours,* service of readings of Friday and Saturday of the tenth week of ordinary time.

toward us;
and the faithfulness of the Lord
endures forever.
Praise the Lord!

Well then, in a few days or a week, you can begin learning another short Psalm. . . . By repeating them, you will, little by little, begin to feel your interior existence suffused with the Spirit of God.

When we pray the Psalms, we have access to the light given by God to guide us through the mists that permeate our uncertain lives, a light which will penetrate those denser patches of shadows made up of refusals and sidestepping. God gives us this light not to cause us to despair, but, on the contrary, to heal and save us; because, simultaneously, Christ will be leading our hearts, which will have become more attentive to his presence, to discover the truth, depth, and beauty of our existence. This is the way to live life in all its human dimension. Otherwise, we become only beasts who spend our days eating, drinking, and looking at television. Such a one never bothers with thinking, is afraid of everything, and closes his eyes and his heart to anything whatsoever. By contrast, faith in God gives even the most timid of us an assurance which surprises no one more than ourselves. Whoever is sure of God, and not of himself, is not afraid to face his own weaknesses and limitations.

Just before falling off to sleep, form with your lips and store in your heart a verse of the Psalm that you have chosen for nourishment, and wake up with it. While you sleep, this presence of the Word of God will search out in the depths of your consciousness all that you may not have succeeded in bringing up to the light of day, and it will be illuminated with the light of God Savior. As you rest, those words will produce fruit, much more than you could ever imagine. Just as Isaiah prophesied (55:11), "So shall my word be that goes forth from my mouth; it shall not return empty, but it shall accomplish that which I purpose, and prosper in the thing for which I sent it." And Jesus says to us, "The Kingdom of God is as if a man should scatter seed upon the ground, and should sleep and rise night and day, and the seed should sprout and grow, he knows not how" (cf. Mark 4:26, 27).

# FOURTH STEP

*Morning:*
*Offer*
*Your Life to God*

If you are like many people, you find it hard to wake up in the morning, you always feel rushed because there is so little time left for getting to work, or maybe you have small children underfoot. In short, mornings are most often disagreeable and hectic times of day. Then why not begin your day, from the moment you open your eyes, by calmly and deliberately tracing the sign of the Cross on yourself and pausing for a moment to reflect on the inexhaustible treasure of its meaning? If you have to be discreet, you can "sign" only your heart, as a secret gesture of gratitude to your Lord. That much, at least, is always possible, for anyone, in all circumstances.

But should one do more? Yes, I think so.

Then how?

* * * *

First of all, a bit of advice: in order to pray in those brief and hurried moments at the beginning of the day, we must often resort to a set form of prayer, repeated in a fixed order—on the condition, of course, that we can avoid succumbing to routine and weariness. But we should not be afraid of repetition or habit per se. Prayer, in fact, requires a different kind of attention from that needed to look at a television program. Television is constantly presenting us with new images to catch the eye, to appeal to and distract our minds. In prayer, on the contrary, the repetition of the same words and the same phrases which are naturally linked can help us to find, with confidence, a true interior freedom. Just as a familiar path allows the hiker to enjoy the scenery because he knows its stones and contour, and his feet adjust instinctively to the slightest change. He can gaze at the sky, peer at a flower along the edge of the path, or greet a fellow hiker.

Repetition and automatic functioning, rather than restricting personal freedom, are, in practice, a necessary condition for the existence and enlargement of that freedom. I would like to point out, by the way, that repetition is one of the fundamental characteristics of the liturgy which has been codified in order to constitute a rite. This codification results in a great freedom for each worshiper because it protects him from the unpredictable, subjective fantasy of the presiding priest. That is *one* of the major differences between liturgical rite and theatrical performance. Many people in the theater have been fascinated by this symbolic power of the liturgical rite, and have never ceased to envy it.

For the morning prayer, then, I suggest that you rely on familiar and repetitive prayers.

You will object, perhaps, saying, "If I simply repeat well-known phrases, I risk just uttering words and not praying with my heart." In reply to this objection, I would now like to consider the practical conditions surrounding morning prayer.

\*   \*   \*   \*

There are three possible situations.

First. You find it possible to set aside some time for prayer, a fairly long time: a half hour, three quarters of an hour, an hour, sometimes more. In addition, you are assured of being able to spend this period in silence and interior freedom. You have decided to give God an ample period of time for prayer. In this case, the Holy spirit can accord you the grace of experiencing the intimate stirring of your spirit which lets itself be seized by God. At times, distressed by your sins and limitations, at other times, filled with joy, you will ask, you will plead, you will contemplate, you will worship. There will be times, too, when you struggle with yourself in darkness. In short, as you "endure" in this way before God, who sees us as we are, the deepest part of your conscience will be awakened, even if only in the whirlwind of the senses and imagination.

Second. You are really pressed for time, and feeling overwhelmed by worries. Are you then just going to give up praying? Certainly not! In this case, you simply must rely on well-known words to support you in those brief moments of attention given to God. It may happen that one day you feel a surge of joy just in thinking about God, or in speaking certain words: "God loves me!" The next day, you may be overcome by sadness: "Jesus, crucified, wished to take on himself all the sin and suffering of the world, in order to deliver us from it." And there you are, if only for a second, with your spirit awakened by the presence of God. All of a sudden, your heart will vibrate, and your love for him will flare up within you: "Christ calls me to follow him, and I want to follow him."

But it can also happen that you are quite simply

exhausted. You have not slept enough. You have to force yourself to get out of bed and to go through all the mechanical motions habitual to the morning. Then, in a flash, you are assailed by yesterday's cares, and by all the things you have to do in the day that is just beginning. You have to set about working, but you have no desire to think or to concentrate. You feel more like a drowsy beast than a conscious and free human being at the dawn of Creation.

In that situation, you must do what I suggested earlier: sing praises to God, bless the Father who loves us, the Son who saves us, the Spirit who lives in our hearts. Also, you can venture as far as uttering words of intercession and contrition. But do it with the aid of set and repetitive phrases. Your prayer need not be mechanical or rote. It can be the free prayer of a man or woman who is admittedly half-asleep and still or already absorbed by cares, but who is, nevertheless, praying resolutely.

Your prayer can be a supremely free act—in spite of your inattention, in spite of the hassle you face every day—because you love.

A comparison. You who are married, who have children, or who have the daily responsibility for another person are sometimes required to do something for one of those persons whom you love at a time when your response is far from wholehearted or enthusiastic because of your fatigue or busy life. But you do it all the same—out of love. Love often consists of acting because one wants to love. The same thing applies in our relationship with God. To keep one's resolution to pray, to repeat well-known prayers expressing thanksgiving and praise—out of love—is a true prayer.

The prayer of the heart is a gift of God which im-
plies a receptive soul or one that God renders receptive. Prayers of the lips often lead to prayers of the
heart, just as prayers of the heart often lead to prayers
of the lips.

Third. You really have no time at all, or you live in
an environment that makes prayer impossible. Then
make the sign of the Cross, in secret if necessary, as I
suggested earlier. Pray mentally while you go through
the routine motions that follow your getting up. Pray
while racing down the stairs, while waiting for the bus,
while riding the subway. Turn your heart toward God,
and repeat your prayer interiorly.

*    *    *    *

I now address myself to those of you who have a
little free time in the morning. I urge you to pause, as
soon as you wake up, and on your knees or standing,
depending on your habitual way of praying, turn yourself toward your crucifix or icon, the holy image in your
room, or else toward the nearest church. Do you know
the direction? If not, turn toward the rising sun, sign of
the resurrected Christ (most churches are, for this reason, oriented toward the Levant, which is also, in our
country, the direction of Jerusalem), and pray.

I can recommend five prayers. Recite them in an
order that you will have decided on beforehand. For
example, pray the *Lord's Prayer,* taught to us by Christ.
Follow it with a *Hail Mary,* in order to pray with the
Virgin. Repeat the *Profession of Faith* in communion
with the entire Church. Continue with *"Glory to the
Father, to the Son and to the Holy Spirit,"* recalling your
baptism, and go on to *"Glory to God in the Highest,"*

the *Gloria* of the Mass (it was originally a morning prayer), thus uniting yourself with the Eucharist being celebrated in the churches around you.

You already know these prayers by heart. If not, have a book in front of you. After a while, you will not need it. Try; it will be easy!

* * * *

Then, in the twinkling of an eye, present God with the day he gives you. It is a grace to live; do you understand me? It is a grace, a gift from God. Life is offered to us; we are not condemned to it. Even if you are in misery or the victim of misfortune, even if you are in prison (I know that prisoners—both men and women— have listened to me on radio), even if you are suffering and asking God to heal you, even if you are facing a day filled with heavy obligations or painful events, you must realize that to live is a precious opportunity that God gives us.

Today, as you live hour by hour—no matter what the obstacles—you still have a bit of freedom left: the freedom of offering to God your decision to live this day committed to returning his love and sharing it with the people you will meet, known and unknown. Just as Christ offers himself to the Father, offer your day to the glory of God, in a "sacerdotal act" since we are, says the Apostle Peter in his first Letter (2:9), ". . . a royal priesthood, a holy nation." In your prayer of praise, you can offer to God, in advance, the day that lies ahead. You can say to him that you wish to hand it over to his love, to submit it to his will. Offer, before they occur, the sufferings and the joys which will mark your day, the decisions which you will have to make or the situa-

tion which will test your fidelity, the exceptional en-
counter as well as the difficult relations with close associates. In other words, live—not like an animal—but
with an awareness of what you are doing. You have
received from God the freedom to act, to live and to
love. Direct that freedom toward him.

\*    \*    \*    \*

Finally, if you have paid close attention to the
scriptural readings of the previous Sunday, or if you
have already prepared those for the forthcoming one,
you may want to memorize a phrase from the Gospels,
or from the Old or New Testaments, which has struck
you and which you have made a note of. Keep that
phrase in your head and in your heart throughout the
week, as you would a refrain which you like to repeat,
or a precious word which finds its echo in you, and little
by little dwells in and penetrates your heart. For example, in the Liturgy of the Word of last Sunday (Septem-
ber 9, 1984), the twenty-third Sunday of Ordinary
Time, these verses from Paul's Letter to the Romans
(13:8–10): "Owe no one anything, except to love one
another," and "Love does no wrong to a neighbor;
therefore, love is the fulfilling of the law." Or else, the
last sentence of the Gospel of Saint Matthew (18:19, 20):
"Again I say to you,"—it is Christ who is speaking, and it
is a beautiful thing to repeat his words to oneself—"if
two of you agree on earth about anything they ask, it
will be done for them by my Father in heaven. For
where two or three are gathered in my name, there am
I in the midst of them."

That phrase, chosen from the Sunday readings, will stay with you all during the week, and from it you will gain your weekly nourishment and the prolongation of the Eucharist in which you had the grace to participate.

# FIFTH STEP

## *Punctuate the Day with Prayer*

How do we go about praying during the day? I have indicated already that the tradition of the Church recommends that we pray seven times a day. Why? First of all, because the people of Israel offered their time to God in seven daily prayers at specific hours, either in the Temple or simply "turned toward him": "Seven times a day I praise thee for thy righteous ordinances" (Psalm 119:164).

The second reason is that Christ himself, faithful to his religious upbringing, prayed that way. And the third reason is that his disciples did, too: the Apostles (cf. Acts of the Apostles 3:1—Peter and John), and the first Christians of Jerusalem were "devoting themselves . . . to the prayers" (cf. Acts of the Apostles 2:42; 10:30—Peter's vision of Cornelius when he went up at the sixth hour to pray). We also have the examples of the early Christian communities and, later, the monastic communities. Today, monks, nuns, and priests are called to recite or sing at seven different times each day the "hours" of the "office." (Office means the "duty," "charge," or "mission" to pray). They pause to sing the Psalms, to meditate the Holy Scriptures, to intercede for human needs and render glory to God. The Church invites all Christians to mark their days—in the spirit of love, faith, and hope—by recurrent, resolute, and deliberate prayer.

* * * *

Because we are God's children in whom the Holy Spirit dwells, we can and must relate to him, not as strangers or as people who ignore him, but as his sons and daughters. We have to get to know our Heavenly Father, and keep alive in our hearts the memory of our completely free and loving relationship with him who is our Creator and Redeemer. We can and must speak to God "as a friend speaks to a friend" and allow his Word to reverberate continuously in our hearts.

Furthermore, by baptism, each Christian is in communion with the entire Church, which prays and supports him in his prayer. Reciprocally, each Christian prays with all the Church and supports every other Christian who prays. Even when we pray in solitude, we are "carried" by all the Church. We are, according to the beautiful expression of Father Hans-Urs von Balthasar, "surrounded and encircled by innumerable co-orants,"[1] and we support all of our brothers and sisters who pray.

Consequently, it is apparent that the duty to pray continuously—"You ought always to pray and not lose heart," Jesus says (Luke 18:1)—is a part of our vocation as members of the Body of Christ. Our heart's perpetual conversation with God, it's crying out and interceding day and night, enlists us in the ecclesiastical dimension of our faith which is common to all Christians. The invitation to pray is addressed to me, personally. I re-

---

[1] *La prière contemplative,* Fayard, 1972, p. 75.

spond in secret, at the place where I am most alone. But in that secret place, precisely, I am in communion with the totality of the universe. With my prayer, I am working with Christ and the Church for the salvation of all men. The young Theresa, secluded and ill in her convent at Lisieux, worked (cf. John 5:36; 10:25; 14:12) in communion with all the Church, which was then in the throes of the dramatic problems of that century; atheism, wars, crimes, and so forth. "It is too little remarked," continues Hans-Urs von Balthasar, "how much the community of saints intervenes in contemplation of a personal and ineffaceably individual nature."[2]

Therefore, we are to pray throughout the day in order to keep ourselves present before God, who is always present to us. The invitation to pray regularly during the day is addressed in particular to those of us who live in a world where the visible signs of faith, its reference points and social rites, are scarcely heard or seen. Most often the Christian—layperson, but sometimes also priest—lives a life of extreme spiritual solitude. He has virtually no occasion to express his faith, nor any tangible means of signifying daily communion in the charity of Christ. He is all alone in carrying the weight of Christian hope. That is still another reason to orient, very deliberately, our attention and our regard toward God.

The call to frequent prayer, however, is a necessity which does not stem from our contemporary situation alone. Jesus teaches his disciples "always to pray and not lose heart" (Luke 18:1). Saint Paul repeats tirelessly

---

[2] Ibid., p. 91.

the injunction of "always praying" (2 Thessalonians
1:11; Philippians 1:4; Romans 1:9; Colossians 1:3;
Philemon 4), and of "not losing heart" (2 Thessalonians
3:13; 2 Corinthians 4:1–16; Galatians 6:9; Ephesians
3:13).

We must be "making the most of the time," as,
again, Saint Paul writes (Ephesians 5:16 and Colossians
4:5).

The indispensability of continuous prayer is taught
to us by the spiritual experience of Israel, by the history
of the people of God, by the tradition of the prayer of
Jesus himself, which is the prayer of the Church.

*   *   *   *

Before deciding if you are going to pray two, three,
four, five, six, or seven times a day, you should heed this
practical suggestion: associate the times of your daily
prayer with the regularly scheduled duties and itiner-
aries that break up your days.

For example, those of you who work during regular
hours always have a short period between the time you
leave home and the time you arrive at work. . . . You
are on foot, or in your car, or in the subway or a bus at
about the same hour every day. And it takes you approximately the same amount of time to get to work
and to return home. Why not set aside those periods for
prayer?

Maybe you are a mother who stays at home, but
you have young children to take to and pick up at
school at set times each day. Use those "breaks" in your
activities for prayer. Another activity that results in a
pause at a relatively precise hour is lunchtime, even if
through necessity or bad nutritional habits you eat only

a sandwich or a quick snack. Why not transform these daily interruptions in your schedule into occasions for brief prayers?

Do by all means pinpoint those fairly regular times in your day when your activities change or, at least, change tempo: the beginning and end of the workday, mealtimes, the commute to and from work, and so forth. And then, faithfully set aside these intervals for prayer, however brief, just long enough perhaps to give a "nod of recognition" to God. But make it a strict obligation, no matter what else happens, to consecrate a prayer to God at that specific time, even if you have no more than thirty seconds or a minute free. Under the attentive eyes of God you will be able to readjust yourself to your different occupations. Your prayer will fortify you for facing the events that you are given to live.

If you are on your way to work, you may find yourself thinking about your colleagues there, of the difficulties that you have to face in an office shared with one or two other persons. The more cramped and routine the working conditions, the more likely personalities are to clash. Ask God, before the working day begins, *"Lord, help me to live today's contact with my fellow workers in a spirit of true charity. Help me to discover the requirements for fraternal love in the light of the Passion of Christ, who will enable me to sustain the effort demanded of me."*

If you work for a large supermarket or department store, you may think about the hundreds of faces that will file past you, without your having the time to look attentively at even one of them. In anticipation, you can say to God, *"Lord, I pray for all those people who are going to rush past me. I am going to try to smile at them, even if I don't have the heart to do it when they are rude and treat me like a calculating machine."*

You should profit as much as you can from the obligatory interruptions and "commutes" in the day, from those occasions when you find yourself with a little extra time. They will allow you, if you are vigilant, a small space of interior freedom where you can catch your breath in the presence of God.

Is it possible to pray on the subway or other public transport? I have done it, using different methods, depending on the times and circumstances of my life. There was a period when I found the noise so bothersome that I used earplugs to isolate myself and achieve a maximum of silence. I prayed this way, but I never cut myself off from the people around me. I was still able to be attentive to them with my eyes, without, however, scrutinizing or staring, or being in any way indiscreet in the way I looked at them. The physical silence allowed me to be even freer in my "welcome." At other times, on the contrary, I had exactly the opposite experience. Each of us does the best he can. But remember, it is always possible to pray wherever you are.

Here is another idea. On your daily route from your subway exit or bus stop to your home or workplace, you will almost certainly be able to find, in Paris at least, a church or a chapel within a radius of three to five hundred meters. By taking a short detour—it will give you the chance to stretch your legs—you can enter that church. Either you will be able to pray peacefully or you will be constantly distracted. Whether the church suits your sensibility or not is another question. In any case, you will be in a church with the Blessed

Sacrament. But, if you prefer, walk a little farther—it may take you ten minutes or so, and the exercise will be good for you—to another church. Go inside and keep walking until you reach the Blessed Sacrament. Kneel and pray—for only ten seconds if that is all the time you can spare. Give thanks to God the Father for the mystery of the Eucharist in which you are included, and for this presence of Christ in his Church. Make yourself a worshiper with Christ, in Christ, by the power of the Holy Spirit. Cross yourself, and be on your way.

What relief this kind of prayer made into a regular practice can bring us after a day when we have been beset by problems or harassed by noise, by the trite content of a persistently blaring radio, by advertising that assaults both our ears and our eyes . . . ! What freedom we can experience in those intervals when we turn with all our being—soul, heart, intelligence—toward something greater than ourselves. The result is that we ourselves become greater because of our attention to the One who is the source of all life and all love!

# SIXTH STEP

*Mealtime (1):*
*Life and Communion*

We must set aside fixed times for prayer, so that our freedom is aided in its resolution to live constantly—or as often as possible—with our thoughts directed toward God. Why is this attention to him so important? Try giving it, and you will understand just how well-founded such advice is. I also appeal to your common sense: if you never think of someone, does it not indicate that you do not love him? Thinking of God is not only a voluntary effort on our part to be attentive to him, but it is also a response to God, who thinks unceasingly of us and who unceasingly supports our existence, who loves us and gives us the strength and the joy to live and to love him.

\* \* \* \*

Here, I would like to talk about some very important fixed times during our days: mealtimes. I want to urge you to make, or to make again, a firm resolution to pray before and after each meal. You who are older will be flooded with memories, probably nostalgic, of the "Bless us, Lord, bless this food . . ." which you heard in your youth. And no doubt, you who are younger will be asking yourselves, "What on earth is he talking about?"

It is a fact that the *"Benedicite"*—after having been extremely important to the most fervent of the generations of the forties and fifties, who considered it a burning obligation—has fallen into disuse in recent decades. We are afraid of seeming artificial; we tend to think of it as a sign of archaic piety—or as simply out of place—in a secularized world emancipated from conventions and social constraints. Basically, we have not known where to situate it or ourselves. I have a confession to make. You might assume, perhaps, that as Archbishop of Paris, I should be able to pray at mealtimes without having to hesitate. However, it often used to happen, when I had guests, that I would ask myself whether I should impose a gesture of prayer on those whom I had invited, even if they were Christians and I knew it. I have subsequently made up my mind on that question, and I exhort you to do the same, for the following reason.

It was not so long ago that mealtime still had a strong symbolic value: it was a sociable event, a time for "life together" and, hence, a time for communication. Sharing the same food, eating the same bread, we came together to sit at the same table. Mealtime is the occasion of a completely vital gathering which marks and influences us throughout our lives: it is the very symbol of communion.

Customs have changed. Today, many of us skip a meal, we eat a quick bite, are satisfied with a sandwich, or, at best, we go to a "snack bar" or a "self."[1] By the way, the word *self* seems to me to have an extraordinary significance. Have you thought about what it means in English? To me, it conveys the message of "each person for himself" for an occasion when a coming together and a sharing might be expected. . . . Eating no longer falls into the category of human rela-

---

[1] A "self-service" restaurant.

tions and communion, but rather comes under the
heading of individual subsistence. The act of eating was
once a community rite which brought together a family, a specific group, or, indeed, an entire village for a
time of essential sharing. But much more than food was
shared: sometimes it was tranquillity, sometimes it was
relaxation, sometimes it was a festivity, but almost always it was a sharing of conversation—since the adults
could talk to one another even if the children had to
keep quiet. In short, even when it was no more than a
necessary action performed together, mealtime was an
excellent time for "life in common." And here it is
today transformed into a strictly individual act.

Even though, because of the evolution of society,
communication at mealtime has ceded its place to biological necessity, the food eaten has acquired a new
importance in contemporary lifestyles. Hunger is
rarely a consideration, as it was some thirty or forty
years ago for great numbers of people. When I was
growing up in Paris, I would get a good scolding if I
wasted even the tiniest crumb of bread. I have a great
nostalgia for that bread, the *"gros pain"* as we called it,
that the *boulangère*—because it was always the baker's
wife who sold it—used to weigh on a Roberval scale,
adding a small piece from another loaf in order to make
the exact weight. (Older Parisians will remember that
practice.) When I was sent to buy the bread, the reward
I had was the right to eat that extra piece, called *la
pesée,* if my memory is correct, on the way home. How
delicious it was, often warm, always crusty, with a flavor
that is not found in bread today.

But enough of these reminiscences: everyone has
his own "madeleine"! . . .

Consider the priority given today to the way we nourish ourselves. Never before has so much attention been given to special diets, general nutrition, weight watching, and so forth. It is as though eating, in becoming an individual act, has found an unprecedented value and emotional connotation: all pay attention to what they eat, even if they eat it on the run.

Whatever the circumstances, eating remains completely necessary in two respects: it is a social act of communion and communication, and it is each person's means of surviving and controlling his life.

\* \* \* \*

Notwithstanding the conditions in which it is eaten, a meal also has a profoundly religious and Christian value. Biblical tradition transmits to us a very rich and powerful symbolism. For human beings, food represents life and death. From the magnificent opening page of the Bible, in the book of Genesis, we understand the coherence and logic of our condition as "creatures" under the eyes of God. In the act of love by which God creates man, in his image and likeness, he entrusts him with all the plants in the Garden of Eden, so that man can feed himself from the edible things that grow from the soil: "Behold, I have given you every plant yielding seed which is upon the face of all the earth, and every tree with seed in its fruit; you shall have them for food" (Genesis 1:29). The world was created in such a way that we can live from it by eating what grows.

The Bible also says, "And the Lord God commanded the man saying, 'You may freely eat of every tree in the garden; but of the tree of the knowledge of good and evil you shall not eat, for in the day that you eat of it you shall die' " (Genesis 2:16, 17). Food, just as much as sexuality, is associated with sin. The eating of the fruit of the Tree of Life clearly illustrates that in the vital function of feeding himself man engages his freedom. It is altogether different for an animal who grazes on grass! From the time of man's creation, food has been charged with a specific value. The initial fault by which man, created in the image and likeness of God, is wounded and falls from his supreme position as creature—or, in other words, king of Creation—has for its particular consequence, "In the sweat of your face shall you eat bread" (Genesis 3:19). From that time on, food is linked with sorrow, suffering, and labor.

The expression "earning a living" connotes "earning money," and more specifically, finding a way to feed both yourself and your family. However, in the Gospel, Jesus says, "For whoever would save his life will lose it; and whoever loses his life for my sake and the gospel's will save it. For what does it profit a man, to gain the whole world and forfeit his life?" (Mark 8:35, 36). In order to survive, man must earn not only materially, but spiritually as well. He must find and conserve the sense, honor, and beauty of his life. When God promises the "holy" Land to Israel—holy because it is there that God will live, give of himself, and communicate with his people—he calls it a "land flowing with milk and honey" (Exodus 3:8), a nourishment which is both human and divine and which will be given to the chosen people so that they can live. All the hardships endured in the desert—the ordeals of fasting, hunger, and distress—demonstrate that man's life is constantly threatened, but that it is again and again restored by

God's gift of the nourishment which comes directly from him: manna (cf. Exodus 16:15).

\* \* \* \*

God communicates his will to the People of Israel through the Covenant. The people receive the law of life so that they can express their adoration of God, and find the meaning of their existence. The Covenant is sealed by sacrifices, true rites of communion. The sacred offering to God is given back, sanctified, to man, who thus partakes of a quasi-heavenly banquet, a foreshadowing of the Messianic Feast fulfilled by Christ and prophesied by Isaiah in these words: "On this mountain the Lord of hosts will make for all peoples a feast of fat things, a feast of wine on the lees, of fat things full of marrow, of wine on the lees well refined. . . . He will swallow up death forever" (Isaiah 25:6–8).

The Resurrection is already announced in this passage from Isaiah, which clearly illustrates the extent of the symbolism of food. Food designates not only the means necessary for physical survival, but it prophesies that life received from God is not limited to earthly existence; it is stronger than death. The prophet Isaiah leads us to understand that by the act of faith with which the people receive their sustenance from God, death will not only be defied, it will be conquered. God will give life, a life that surpasses the life of the body already marked by death. He will give us a life that triumphs over the power of death.

Jesus, who during his forty days in the desert passes through the trials of fasting and hunger, is tempted by Satan: "If you are the Son of God, command those stones to become loaves of bread" (Matthew 4:3). Jesus,

the Messiah, the Son of the living God, answers by cit-
ing a passage from Deuteronomy (8:3): "It is written,
'Man does not live by bread alone, but by every word
that proceeds from the mouth of God.'" Later, Jesus
feeds a multitude of people who follow him to a de-
serted spot by multiplying the five loaves of bread,
which prophesies another nourishment: his flesh and
his blood shed for us (cf. John 6). Before his Passion,
Jesus celebrates the Passover rite with his disciples and
says, "Take this, all of you, and eat it: this is my body
which will be given up for you. . . . Take this, all of
you, and drink from it: this is the cup of my blood, the
blood of the new and everlasting covenant. It will be
shed for you and for all so that sins may be forgiven. Do
this in memory of me."

Thus, in this exemplary manner, we are led to
grasp the spiritual reality of which the meal becomes
the sign: two aspects which make only one, a bringing
together by God, or better still, communion with God
and life received from God.

# SEVENTH STEP

*Mealtime (2):*
*Giving Thanks to God*

To fortify our willpower and good intentions, we should recall the command that Jesus gave us: "You ought always to pray." Much of the time we live as though we were leaves being swept away by the wind or pebbles being thrust forward in a torrent. We are snatched this way and that by the currents of life around us—its habits, its customs, its fads. Every day we are subjected to the innumerable and often oppressive demands of life in a big city. We are assailed by blatant advertising, by the obsessive repetition of the news, by stress originating from multifarious sources: within the same day we may find ourselves having to race for a train in the subway corridors, and later, having to sit motionless and lose precious time in a traffic tie-up. Moreover, in the climate of artificiality which characterizes our civilization, references to our faith have been diminished, indeed, sometimes deliberately blotted out. However, the challenge of faith is all the more urgent in such a world.

In the midst of the circumstances of our pressured existence, we must preserve a margin of freedom where the true orientation of our lives can manifest itself. We need to be purer, more vigorous, stronger, and more vigilant in affirming our faith. God is not a part of the exterior scenery: he comes to us in the deep-

est part of our being, our freedom; he gives us the
assurance of his presence in the sacraments of Christ.
But it remains for us to consent to reserving that secret,
innermost place within ourselves and to meeting God
there.

Prayer at the beginning and end of a meal is a
privileged occasion for such a meeting. Formerly it, as
well as other Christian practices, marked these times of
day. In the country, for example, the father of the family would take the loaf of bread and, before slicing it,
trace the sign of the Cross on it with the knife. What
nobility and beauty such gestures have! And yet, they
have virtually disappeared from our lives. For me, they
call to mind that poetic profession of faith by Claudel:
"I sowed my wheat and I reaped it, and in this bread
made by me, all my children have received communion" *(L'annonce faite à Marie).*

It is up to us who live in Christ, Word of God present at the Creation, Lamb of the Banquet of the Apoca-
lypse, to restore the full spiritual significance to the
daily nourishment we take. Prayer at mealtime is one of
the reference points inscribed in our human condition.
But what content do we give to this prayer in the epoch
of the sandwich, the snack bar, and nutritional obses-
sions carried to the extreme?

I will say only one thing: we must bless God for the
food he gives us; beyond that, we can bless God, give
him thanks, express our joy to him, our gratitude. We
can thank him for permitting us to live, for giving us
hope of life, even if that life is sometimes bitter to us.
Bless God for the gifts he gives us, the most precious of
which is the gift he makes of himself as Father who
wants us to be his children, his sons and daughters,

through Creation and Redemption. Bless God for the Son whom he gives to us and to whom we have become similar by baptism in his death and Resurrection. Bless God for his Holy Spirit who lives in our hearts. Give him thanks that we are able to receive his nourishing gifts, the fruits for which we, mankind, have toiled and struggled, by which, nevertheless, come from him. It is not a question of blessing the food, but of blessing God for the fact that we can eat and receive life, a life that has meaning! Bless him for giving us food in such a way that we are united with Jesus, who says, "My food is to do the will of him who sent me, and to accomplish his work" (John 4:34).

*     *     *     *

What words should we use? Perhaps we might consider the short prayer of the Offertory in the ritual of the Mass: "Blessed are you, Lord God of all Creation. Through your goodness we have this bread to offer, which earth has given and human hands have made. . . ." Here we have a liturgical expression which presents us with an excellent structure for a prayer of thanksgiving to God before and after a meal. It is actually the Jewish blessing for daily meals, and Jesus spoke it every day. Other than it, there is an infinite variety of appropriate prayers in the tradition of the Church. You can invent your own, or else choose some that are already made, from long ago or more recent times, and learn them. You can also—and it is just as good—let a thought that has been close to your heart all day well up from inside you, or you can repeat a phrase from the Gospel or the Scriptures, sing a song of praise from the Psalms. I have already suggested that you learn Psalm

117. Leaf through your Psalter, and you will be able to glean many other relevant verses. For example, Psalm 103:1, 2:

> "Bless the Lord, O my Soul;
> and all that is within me,
> bless his holy name.
> Bless the Lord, O my Soul
> and forget not all his benefits."

Psalm 108:4, 5:

> "For thy steadfast love is great above
> the heavens,
> thy faithfulness reaches to the clouds.
>
> Be exalted, O God, above the
> heavens!
> Let thy glory be over all the earth!"

Psalm 133:1:

> "Behold, how good and
> pleasant it is
> when brothers dwell together in unity!"

You should also look at Psalms 134, 135, 146 to 150, as well as these final words in the Psalter (Psalm 150:6):

> "Let everything that breathes
> praise the Lord!
> Praise the Lord!"

\*   \*   \*   \*

When we are blessing God for all the gifts he gives us, we should keep in mind the two aspects of eating which I pointed out in the last step: life and communion.

Eating is, first of all, an act by which we personally receive life for our body. It is fitting, then, in these circumstances, to bless God for life—life given, received, and sustained thanks to the food before us. But we also bless God for our life which has been delivered from sin and death. This true life, "eternal" life, unites us with God, and already it gives our body its dignity, its beauty, and its hope. Through this life, we discover the grandeur of man in his bodily existence, because that which distinguishes man from God's other creatures is that he has been made in the image and likeness of God.

Secondly, the content of the prayer at mealtime must refer to our solidarity with all mankind. In the act of eating, an act that so often brings men together, I can by a personal prayer enter into communion with all humanity. Even if I am eating alone, hurriedly, just to nourish myself, I can express my solidarity with others, and united with Christ, I can rejoin the hoped-for communion with the totality of mankind: those who have enough to eat and those who are dying of hunger, those I love and know and those I do not know, but who are seated around me, those I hear speaking now and those I heard speaking earlier today. Let mealtime become an act of communion which gives you the freedom to rejoin all of those people to whom you have been given and all of those who have been given to you.

Having understood this, how does a person proceed? In particular, if he is eating in a self-service or other public dining place. I have no spiritual recipes, as I warned you earlier. I can only pass on several possibilities based on experiences which have been confided to me, which I have observed, or which I have had personally.

First situation. You are in the company restaurant, in a cafeteria—no matter where, but away from home. Some people dare, calmly and without either provocation or embarrassment, to make the sign of the Cross, and then to pause and pray inwardly, because they believe that it is their duty. You have to have grace and courage to do this, but I have never seen people laugh or mock it; generally, it elicits a certain respect.

You can also borrow a custom from the Germanic peoples who, once seated at table, observe a short period of silence, giving each person the time to pray in the intimacy of his heart, to collect his thoughts and give thanks to God. However short it may be, such a space in the wall of our exterior concerns and preoccupations—a breach where God can slip in—can reorient us toward the meaning of our existence.

So pray in silence; if possible, make a discreet sign of the Cross. I have often signed my heart and lips without being noticed by my neighbor. All of us have a need to give ourselves these special signs, and we have certain instinctive gestures to which we normally pay no attention. However, even our general hearing, even our physical expressions must be submitted to the love of Christ. They can help us to think of him and to give thanks to him. It is always feasible to take a brief instant to pray before you begin to eat. Suppose you have brought your tray to a table, and you stand over it for a few seconds before sitting down. Will those around you think that you are daydreaming? So what? You are not dreaming, but praying for them. All of a sudden, by your praying presence you are introducing into the hubbub of modern life, into the act of eating which has become automatic, into the daily humdrum and lassitude of your existence, the presence of the power of Christ and the liberating act of Redemption.

\*   \*   \*   \*

Still another situation. You are at home with your family—with your children, young or almost grown, alone with your spouse, with other relatives, or with close friends. If everybody agrees, then pray together. For that, you must take some time. There is nothing more ridiculous than a hastily spoken prayer when words are mumbled for the sake of repeating words. It is that kind of prayer which annoys and becomes meaningless because it is nothing more than a routine. Allow yourself time for a real pause, for real spiritual respiration, for real peace. If some members of the family are not believers, you can show your respect for them by saying beforehand something like this: "Listen, some of us here are going to pray. While we give thanks to God, you can profit from a little interior silence and calm down. We'll pray for you. Since we are here to share this food prepared together, or that some of us have prepared for others, let's share a moment of peace, reconciliation, and joy as well. Let's turn ourselves to God, and then to each other, having a good look at each face around the table before we sit down. Hey, why are you looking so upset? What's the matter? Did something go wrong this morning, today? . . ."

Pay attention to each other and you will pay attention to God; you will ask his pardon for yourself and the others; you will give him thanks for bringing you together and allowing you to share the food before you.

*    *    *    *

By introducing a deliberate gesture of prayer into our everyday life, we express our faith, and at the same time, we help each other to live in faith. Beware, however, of letting the grace deteriorate into something mechanical or a kind of imposed obligation—that can be costly. When entered into freely by children of God, the mealtime blessing can become a very solid spiritual reference point. All the more so since, for large numbers of men and women, a meal is "sacred" in the sense that they never want to pass it up, no matter what. You can attach to this vital necessity a voluntary step toward conversion to God, thus reminding yourself that "Man shall not live by bread alone, but by every word that proceeds from the mouth of God" (cf. Matthew 4:4). And you will be cooperating with the work of Christ, the "Way," who opens up the true way by which we have access to the Father, making us God's children—dignified, free, and truthful in love.

# EIGHTH STEP

*Evening (1):*
*The Examination*
*of Conscience*

Here we are at evening. What kind of prayer should it be? I confess, I am embarrassed. I hesitate to propose such and such a way of praying. All of us lead harassed lives, and it is precisely at the end of the day that many people find the greatest difficulty in praying. The accumulated physical and mental fatigue weighs down our freedom. Moreover, individual situations vary widely. Perhaps you live alone; you are of a certain age; your family are scattered—possibly far away; maybe you are a widow or a widower. Or perhaps you are young, unmarried. Or a celibate: layman, nun, or priest. Or separated from your husband, your wife. Although solitude in the evening can be a very precious thing, there are times when it can be hard to endure, even when it has been chosen or accepted. There are others among you who live with your families, and living conditions (especially in Paris) do not make it easy to find either a time or a place for peace and silence.

For all these reasons I speak with circumspection and in all modesty and respect regarding the difficulties a person can have in praying in the evening. First of all, I ask you to forgive me if certain of my proposals are not applicable to your situation. That remark applies, besides, to everything I have previously said about prayer. I am simply passing on to you my own experience and that of numerous other Christians. It has never entered my mind that the advice I have given, even with an air of assurance, should be followed to the letter. Rather, it has been given in the form of suggestions by someone who tries his best to live up to the command and call of God. You, in turn, should feel free to use my suggestions or not. You must respond in the best way that you can to the call which God addresses to you.

How is it possible to consecrate to God, through prayer, those precious but, after all, fragile times at the end of the day? Before getting to the heart of the matter, I would like to envisage several different situations, beginning with the case of those who live in families.

If you are husband and wife, praying together can be a beautiful thing. It is, however, difficult even when both are believers: constraints, a lack of mutual freedom, and routine can set in very quickly. Couples who have tried the evening prayer in common realize, too, that they must remain entirely respectful of each other without becoming a party to a spouse's weakness, or lenient toward one's own. A good rule to follow is to agree in advance on the development of a vocal prayer; make it fixed and relatively short. Let everything concerned with the spontaneous dialogue be optional. Two people can love each other and even grow closer by looking at their life objectively without necessarily having their sensibilities attuned to the point of allowing for the kind of exchanges that sometimes take place in a prayer group, for example. The best guarantee of maintaining a common time for prayer is the reliance on a simple framework, a brief text with a minimum of gestures chosen together in advance. Another time, I shall talk about prayer with children—when they are small and when they are growing up.

It is also beautiful when one member of the family ventures to say—to his spouse or, indeed, to his children: "Okay, I need fifteen minutes of silence—or five minutes of peace. Just leave me alone and let me have a bit of breathing space. My solitude is my secret garden." Certain people have described this to me, and I marvel at it! In difficult material conditions, especially in cramped quarters, it is important that family members—between and among themselves, even if not everyone takes part—respect one another's wishes for a time of silence and peace, a time to pull oneself together. In such circumstances, obviously the best, love and mutual tolerance are of such a quality that each person can let his desire for silence and retreat be known without offending others.

Frequently, however—which is not to say that the people involved do not love each other or else love insufficiently—such a revelation is not possible, and hence, neither is an isolation observed or known about by other members of the family. In that case, you may be obliged to move up the hour of your evening prayer by scheduling it for the time you leave work; or you may be able to profit from a furtive moment of peace at home before other members of the family return. You can also simply postpone your prayer until the hour when everyone is theoretically asleep—that is, when everyone seems to be asleep—and in that secret "space," find yourself before God.

Whatever the circumstances of your life (weariness, physical exhaustion, painful solitude, an uncooperative family), rather than clashing with them as though they were insurmountable obstacles, arrange your life in such a way that, instead of hindering, these obstacles become part of the stimulus for your evening prayer. It is a time for all those who are connected by family ties or life in common to demonstrate spiritual solidarity between and among themselves.

*  *  *  *

At this time, I would like to emphasize an essential element of the evening prayer. Some of you are acquainted with and still practice it. It is a matter of recollecting in God's presence the day we have just lived through, and trying to see with God's light in what ways we have been faithful or unfaithful to his commandments and his love. This very important practice is called "an examination of conscience" in the Christian tradition; it is better known to some people as a "reappraisal of life." Never mind what you call it, but the reality that it encompasses is of the utmost seriousness. Nothing less than the truth and faithfulness of our Christian existence are at stake in this kind of prayer.

I am well aware that many of us have reservations about this kind of prayer. I say "us" on purpose, because it was out of the experience of my generation—perhaps others as well—that these hesitations grew. Our upbringing—an underdeveloped appreciation of what it means to be a child of God, overly precise rules, excessively strict obligations—led many people to feel, and to admit to themselves, that they were being suffocated by burdensome compulsions. But however unpleasant —possibly even searing—these memories are, they must not blind us to the fundamental dimension of our Christian freedom or lead us to evade the responsibility for our conduct. If that happens, we risk living like animals (I have made this point already), so much immersed in the here and now that we never take a moment for interior recollection; nor do we even remember anything about what we have done. Purely and simply carried away by fantasies and fleeting impressions, we become incapable of making a judgment on what we have done, said, or thought; on events and people we have met; in short, on our lives. At that stage, then, do we really have even a minimum of freedom left?

When you are jammed into a subway at rush hour, you cannot move, you have no freedom of action. The body, in order to be able to move in one direction or another, needs free space, certain distances between itself and others. The same is true for all our being, for our entire existence. We can also find ourselves jammed in spiritually by surrounding sensations and stimulations, by a rapid pace of life, by pressures from our work, and so forth. The result is that we keep our minds focused on what we have to do at any one moment, and we never take the time to be truly responsible. That means that we do not really answer for what we are doing or deciding.

\*  \*  \*  \*

Answer to whom? Responsible to whom? To God, who calls us. The responsibility for our acts, which is the guarantee of our authentic freedom, consists in our hearing God call us by our names, and our answering him as though we were at the dawn of Creation: "Adam?" "Here I am." Each one of us should be able to answer the Lord's call in the words of the Virgin Mary:

"Behold, I am the handmaiden of the Lord; let it be to me according to your word." And then, keep our word!

The examination of conscience introduces into our day-to-day existence a distance which allows us to become responsible for our acts by accepting to look at our behavior in the light of God's tenderness. This part of the evening prayer, which helps us to take stock of our lives, when undertaken in an attitude of thanksgiving and confidence in God, is a far cry from an exacerbation of a guilty conscience. It is not a matter of asking oneself, "What good have I done?" "What did I do wrong?" It entails going much deeper and praying:

"Lord, already a few more hours of my life have disappeared, still another day has gone by. I am going to try to tell you how it went. You know already, but I don't see it clearly yet. Please light my day with your light. I want to turn to you. I want to understand your will for me. I want to look back on my day and recall what it was that you were expecting of me; and I want to regain my true freedom by daring to say to myself and to you, 'Today you called me. Today you asked me to do your will. Did I pay attention to your call? Yes, or no? Have I responded to your love? Yes, or no? Yes, Lord, I did what you were asking of me. Thank you, Lord; you permitted me to do something that I didn't think I'd be able to do,' or, 'No, Lord, today I didn't manage. I was a shirker. Have mercy on me; I am a sinner. Forgive me, Lord. I lived like a robot; I don't remember anything. Give me the strength to remember my days so that they don't swirl away like water or dissipate themselves like smoke. Let me live fully. Lord, since you have given me life, let me live to love you. Don't let my feelings become like fleeting clouds or dust, mere playthings for the wind. Don't let my life be consumed by ephemeral concerns, all in vain, for nothing. Let it be inscribed, day after day, in the eternity of your love.' "

\* \* \* \*

With confidence in God, in his goodness and his tenderness, we can take the hours of the day just ending and present them to him who loves us. We can let him shed his truth on our lives and give us the courage to keep on going. The Bible contains a wealth of practical indicators to help us along the way.

• First of all, there are the seven Psalms of conversion and penitence. The Tradition of the Church has reserved them for the expression of the attitude of a heart that turns itself toward God and entrusts itself to him, with its full weight of good and bad. They are:

Ps. 6:    "O Lord, rebuke me not in thy anger";
Ps. 32:   "Blessed is he whose transgression is forgiven";
Ps. 38:   "O Lord, rebuke me not in thy anger";
Ps. 51:   "Have mercy on me, O God, according to thy steadfast love; according to thy abundant mercy, blot out my transgressions";
Ps. 102:  "Hear my prayer, O Lord; let my cry come to thee!";
Ps. 130:  "Out of the depths I cry to thee, O Lord!";
Ps. 143:  "Hear my prayer, O Lord; give ear to my supplications!"

These Psalms are exceedingly beautiful. While you are getting used to looking at your days in the tenderness of God, you may want to repeat only one of them, allowing time for respiration, for silence, and for meditating on a verse that may have evoked a memory or illustrated an event in your day.

• Next, I remind you of the Ten Commandments. They are not just the title of an American movie with a cast of thousands! They are the actual expression of the holiness of God which is shared with the people of the Covenant (Exodus 20:1–17; Deuteronomy 5:6–21). Christ refers us again and again to these "Ten Words" which convey the will of the Father for us, and which he, the Son of God made man, fulfills perfectly.

\*   \*   \*   \*

By applying standards of holiness inspired by God, we situate ourselves, not in relation to a judgment that we or others make of ourselves, but rather in relation to the will of the Heavenly Father. How liberating this act of faith is! In sum, we "examine" the way we have lived, not as a function of guilt feelings or a good or bad conscience, but as a function of the plan that God has for mankind. Actually, it is the only plan for us, because it alone gives us the possibility of attaining God and happiness at the same time.

# NINTH STEP

*Evening (2):*
*Under the Eyes of God*

*"You ought always to pray."* We fulfill this command-ment of Christ when we "weigh up," under his eyes, the events of the ending day. Some of you may be so exhausted by that time or lead such a hectic life that you are incapable of recalling in the evening what has happened during the day. However, by reviewing in prayer a day that we have tried to live in prayer, we step out of the mindlessness of a purely animal life; we also escape our changing moods and shifting emotions which toss us about like clouds or leaves carried away by even the slightest wind. One day we feel depressed and sad; one day we feel elated, without really knowing why.

An interior distance, which I spoke about last week, will allow us to recapture our days through mem-ory and, thus, to regain possession of our lives. We must acquire the capacity to remember what has happened in our days, not to evoke nostalgia or a vague melan-choly—or a sterile regret—but for the purpose of main-taining our capability to act responsibly, to have a fu-ture, and to stay the course of fidelity. Do you remember what Saint Luke reported about the Virgin, after Jesus' birth as well as after his disappearance at the Temple? "But Mary kept all these things, ponder-ing them in her heart" (Luke 2:19, 51).

Of course, Mary was pondering the events that, through her Son, Jesus Christ, were to lead to our salvation. The key to the mystery will be given to her, and to us, in the Passion and Resurrection of Christ and by the gift of the Holy Spirit. Mary kept in mind all those things that were the actual work of God in Jesus. When we pray each evening, we, too, recall the events in our redeemed lives: God's work in us through Jesus. It is in our day-to-day existence that Christ saves us. The sense of what we are living through is revealed to us when we meditate the Word of Christ himself and are associated with his life through the sacraments.

\* \* \* \*

"Reclaiming" our days under God's eyes—without deploring what has happened or regretting what might have been, but rather, by asking forgiveness for our sins and giving thanks for blessings received—is an act of faith in God, who is always active in our lives. There is no life, no moment of any life, that is insignificant. God is always paying attention. If we, in turn, pay attention to what God has given us to live, hour by hour, day by day, if we pay attention to the people we have been able to meet and to ourselves, then we are looking at that part of ourselves which God is looking at. Because even though we are often distracted and unaware, God, who created us and calls us to live in constant communion with him, is constantly with us because he loves us.

When I examine my day under his eyes, I discover it *through* his eyes and receive the grace of having my eye become the "lamp" of my body by letting itself be suffused with God's light. Then my entire body becomes full of his light, and I see more clearly what I am (cf. Luke 11:33–36).

We can begin to live in the brightness of the Covenant of God with his people by welcoming his commandments, receiving them as a Word of God, a revelation of God, and not, as they are still too often regarded, as a series of prohibitions, of arbitrary or repressive prescriptions. The Law of God is not to be compared to human laws.

When God commands something of us, he begins by introducing himself: "I am the Lord your God who brought you out of the land of Egypt, out of the house of bondage" (Exodus 20:2). Furthermore, in reminding us that he has lifted us up from servitude and delivered us from the slavery of sin, God reveals to us who we are. And when these commandments of God are spoken to us later by the Christ-Messiah, notably in the Sermon on the Mount, it is of primordial importance that we receive them in the context of our precise relationship to God: it is God who takes the initiative and who saves us.

Consequently, we can make our own the Psalmist's profession of faith: "I delight in thy law" (Psalm 119:70). He is the delight of someone who is directing his life toward the fulfillment of God's will for him. Jesus himself, in coming into the world, said along with the Psalmist, "I have come to do thy will, O God" (Letter to the Hebrews 10:7). And he explains in the Gospel according to Saint John (4:34): "My food is to do the will of him who sent me, and to accomplish his work." And he replies to the Tempter with words from Deuteronomy: "Man shall not live by bread alone, but by every word that proceeds from the mouth of God" (Matthew 4:4).

The commandments of God are the revelation of God's plan for my life. God alone can teach me to see where my responsibility lies, because he has taken the responsibility for my life by calling me into existence. It is he who gives my life its true value since, having created me in his image and likeness, he has saved me through his beloved Son. In that light, I can more easily distinguish sin from faults in my character. We are the way we are. Our failings, although frequently more irritating for our neighbor than ourselves, also become a source of dissatisfaction for us when we do not accept ourselves as we are. Often the person trying to change his "look" is simply not satisfied with the one the Lord has given him. The face of a man or woman, however, is essentially shaped from the interior, not from the exterior by the skills of a plastic surgeon. We have to accept our character traits with all their weaknesses and limitations—and their riches, too—just as we accept our faces or hair color.

We do have to be on guard, all the same, lest our character traits lead our freedom astray and cause us to sin. Included among them are tendencies and drives that are constant and normal for a human being: agressiveness, sensuality, acquisitiveness, desires of all kinds. We have to learn to cope with these fundamental drives by exercising our freedom. We have to master them and, sometimes, to sublimate them; in any case, to use and integrate them into our personal existence. Our God-given freedom—the fine point of our being, the heart of our heart where our intelligence finds its satisfaction—is capable of dominating the totality of our existence, including our poor bodies with their servitudes, their limits, and their sufferings.

\*   \*   \*   \*

It is essential, then, to distinguish character failings —drives and tendencies—from sin, that is to say, from behavior that engages our responsibility. Responsibility vis-à-vis what? Not just to an ideal that I may have, not just to myself or to my neighbor and the promise I may have given him. We assume our responsibility vis-à-vis the responsibility that God took in creating us and permitting us to share the free and holy action which is his. In the light of God's commandments—his plan for me and for all men—my life, even if it is restricted, seems beautiful and full of meaning since God is always there waiting for me to respond to his call.

Many people ask themselves with anguish: How am I going to serve? What am I going to become? I dare to say to each of you that every life is infinitely precious because every life is unique and carries its own secrets, which cannot be revealed by a fortune-teller or an astrologist. Certainly, on Judgment Day we shall know what we shall have become, as Saint John says in Revelation. Then we shall be given a "white stone with a new name written on the stone which no one knows except him who receives it" (Revelation 2:17). It is useless to try to learn this secret prematurely: God constructs it from day to day through our faithfulness and his pardon, because he is himself faithful.

The irreplaceable character of every human life is that you—Peter, Annette, each of us, each of the billions of men and women on earth—are called to love because you are loved by God. God, three times holy, who created us in the Son, and who, in the Spirit, shapes us into his image and likeness. Not with the expectation that we should all march to the same drummer like toy soldiers. No. In every person whom he calls to live his life, God wants to manifest, for everyone, his supreme Beauty and the splendor of an existence lived in communion with him. The holiness of each human life, unique in God's eyes, is—in the mystery of the communion of saints—necessary to all persons, whoever they are. Sin expresses itself in our lives by a "No" to the commandments of love that have been entrusted to us by God. These commandments define the truth of our task, of our human "job"—or better still, of our vocation in the world: we are to be "perfect, as your heavenly Father is perfect" (Matthew 5:48). Each human being is irreplaceable in the accomplishment of God's holy will, which we fulfill only if we are united with Christ through the faith and the strength of the Holy Spirit.

One last bit of advice: never let yourself become bitter in facing your failings, or nostalgic over an unattainable ideal. We are not required to reach God as an ideal; it is God who reaches down to us. In his Son, he came to touch our deepest abyss. Jesus identified himself with us, not by becoming a sinner, but by making himself sin so that our search for him can begin at the precise point where we are, just as Paul wrote to the Christians in Corinth: "We beseech you on behalf of Christ, be reconciled to God. For our sake he made him to be sin who knew no sin, that in him we might become the righteousness of God" (2 Corinthians 5:20, 21).

You are in God's hands. Do not lose heart in confronting the same struggles over and over, the same weaknesses again and again. Such is life! Just like having to get up in the morning and to go to sleep at night. Of course you have the right to be tired sometimes, but you also have the duty to take heart again. It is such a joy to live! You disagree? Oh, how much I hope that the life you are—or will be—reviewing under God's eyes will bring you the taste of happiness! Did you understand? I said, the taste of happiness. You may protest, "Yes, I heard what you said, but I am so unhappy." Listen, you may be sad, perhaps even afflicted, but happiness is the bliss that God gives: "Blessed are those who mourn, for they shall be comforted. Blessed are the pure in heart, for they shall see God."

Ask God to purify you. Along with the Psalmist, entreat him: *"Create in me a clean heart, O God, and put a new and right spirit within me. A broken and contrite heart, O God, thou wilt not despise"* (Psalm 51:10, 17). With a contrite and purified heart you will experience the utterly inexpressible hope of seeing God, and hence, you can with Christ let yourself fall into a deep and untroubled sleep.

# TENTH STEP

*Evening (3):*
*Pray for Others*

By praying in the evening, we place ourselves in God's perspective and try to look back on our day in the peace and love that he gives us. I have already talked about the examination of conscience or the reappraisal of life. If it suits your temperament, your way of living and feeling, I invite you now to look at the ending day in a systematic and careful way, virtually hour by hour. Such a prayer prevents our lives from slipping away into emptiness and vapidity. When you are bringing back to mind what has happened since you got up in the morning, your prayer may sound something like this:

*Lord, your will for me, I know, is not like that of a human superior. When I go to work, I have to follow the orders of whoever hired me: "Do it this way. Get busy on that." Your will for me, Lord, is altogether different. It is not like an order that I don't understand, because you give me your Holy Spirit, who guides me to an interior understanding and teaches me to love you and desire your will for my life. In confiding your will to me, you once again engage your responsibility. You have already taken on a responsibility for me, much more than my mother and father took in bringing me into the world. You have not only willed that I be born, and given me the joy of living [I repeat, the joy of living, even when life is painful and difficult], but in creating me you took the risk of entrusting me with the freedom to respond to or ignore your unceasing call. I realize, Lord, that your will is not a fatality which is imposed on me: it is rather the condition of my freedom.*

*In return, Lord, I want to thank you for my freedom and assume my responsibility toward you who have assumed such a great responsibility toward me. I am going to do that by giving you an hour-by-hour account of how I spent my day. It is not toward myself that I turn, but toward you, Lord, who are always with me and sustain my life.*

When I pray in this spirit, I am not limited to presenting a kind of "balance sheet" for the day. I also weigh up and accept the responsibility for my life tomorrow, if God grants me a tomorrow. Therefore, when similar circumstances occur, when I find myself once again confronted by my neighbor or fellow workers, or when I meet the same problems in my material, moral, or spiritual life or face the same choices, I can— despite my faintheartedness or fatigue, my temptations or weaknesses, or, on the contrary, because of my unflagging efforts, my generosity and my faithfulness, that is, all the qualities that make up the mystery and beauty of each life—find a point of anchorage because of what I will have understood from my evening prayer.

*Lord, as I have reviewed the difficulties I faced, the decisions I made, and the persons I dealt with today, you have given me the light to see my weaknesses and*

*my sins as well as my faithfulness. When I find myself
in comparable situations in the future, please grant me
even more vigorously the strength of your Holy Spirit,
since through your Son you have made me your child.*

In the retrospect of an ending day which prepares
us for the days to come, we can pray for all those persons, living and dead, who have had a place in our
hearts. And we do that especially on All Saints' Day,
and on All Souls' Day, which is linked with it in the
chronology of the Catholic calendar. Both celebrations
are rich in overtones which cause the glory of human
history to reverberate in all its depth. It is a history
composed of innumerable lives, not one of which is
forgotten by God, and all of which we are charged to
remember in Christ.

We keep the memory of the men and women who
have preceded us not just by recalling their names but,
in the first place, by finding them again in the memory
of God. We who participate in the life of the unique
Son, who are led by the Spirit, have access through the
"Communion of Saints" to the memory of God. I am
not referring exclusively to the praise we address to the
recognized and canonized saints, who are completely
filled with the holiness of God and delivered from everything within themselves that opposes life. As a "holy
nation" (cf. 1 Peter 2:9), we can also celebrate all the
other saints whom we will never know, who will never
be canonized. In a word, we can celebrate all the living
and the dead with whom we are in real communion
because all of us make a single body, the body of Christ
resurrected from the dead, all of those whom Saint Paul

refers to already as "the saints" (cf., for example, Romans 1:7; Ephesians 1:1; Philippians 1:1; 4:21, 22; etc.).

The prayer for everybody—for family members, acquaintances, people you greet and those you do not greet, those you love and those you do not love—is the "ordinary" prayer of intercession with which we are charged. This prayer for our brothers, for whom we are the priests, "a royal priesthood" (cf. 1 Peter 2:9), can easily be integrated into the examination of conscience and the review of our day. How?

First, by an appeal to the pardon and mercy of God, as Christ taught us by his words and his acts. If I am thinking of such and such a person, in such and such a situation, I must ask God to pardon me for the harm I have done to him. That does not dispense me from trying, starting the next day if I can, to make amends or act differently. Even if my faults are such that I am constantly having to struggle with myself, or if the faults of the other person are such that they provoke the same predicament over and over, the fact remains that responsibilities are responsibilities; and if a wrong is committed, it still remains a wrong, regardless of the circumstances.

So we ask God to pardon us for the harm we have done to our brothers. We also ask him to instill in our hearts the mercy, tenderness, peace, and sensitivity of love necessary for us to pardon, and not reproach, our brother for a wrong he may have done to us. That is not easy! But we must ask for it all the same. Notice that I am not saying that you must pardon; I am saying that you must ask God for the strength to pardon, just as Christ did on the Cross: "Father, forgive them; for they know not what they do" (Luke 23:34). That prayer is

particularly difficult for a man being put to death! The
Lord Jesus put that prayer in our hearts so that it will
germinate and do its work and, perhaps, in time, rise to
our lips.

*  *  *  *

Afterward, while thinking about our brothers—
known and unknown, and even our enemies—we must
ask God to grant them the "best" of all destinies, and
we must pray that they will receive and retain it because they will have recognized that it is the best. This
best of gifts, after all, has a name: it is called the Holy
Spirit. This definition was not invented by me; it is Jesus
Christ who defines it, regarding prayer, precisely: "If
you then who are evil know how to give good gifts to
your children, how much more will the Heavenly Father give the Holy Spirit to those who ask him!" Saint
Luke specifies "Holy Spirit" (11:13), Saint Matthew says
"good things" (7:11)

Yes, we must pray that open and receptive hearts
will be ready to welcome the gift that God wants to
make to every man, so that he can find his vocation as a
child of God, and live it fully. As a human being, I am
meant to live in solidarity with all my human brothers
—even if a situation is psychologically blocked, even if a
language barrier exists, even if we are complete strangers. As Christians we can do something—at least mysti-
cally, spiritually—because of our sacerdotal vocation as
God's people. At least, we can pray. And that prayer is
effective: it changes people's relations with one another; and while respecting absolutely the mystery of
each person, it is capable of rendering a person's freedom more receptive to God.

Certain well-meant gestures we make toward others can impose on or offend them. However, this prayer for my brother asks God to restore him to the most authentic and beautiful state of freedom, to open his heart, to bring him peace, to bestow on him what is best for him. When we pray in this way, we can allow all that has hurt us, indeed all that has attacked us in our cruel world and indifferent civilization, to pass over our minds and memories without letting ourselves be crushed by despair over so much misery or overwhelmed by indignation in the face of so many injustices in the world. It is wiser, however, not to reread the newspaper or look at the late evening news on television, which would probably upset us even more and might prevent us from making an act of faith in the goodness of God. But, inversely, without distress or despondency—but also without blindness—we can pray for all of humanity, which is so often miserable and at times so murderous, so steeped in lies and egoisms, so unconcerned about people's fates, so often brutal to the small and weak and, so shamelessly disrespectful of the human condition. You must, my Christian brothers and sisters who can pray, grant men their dignity as children of God by uniting yourself with the intercessory prayer, the sacerdotal prayer of Christ, Son of God made man.

It is a true prayer when we say in the evening: "Lord, you have made me a Christian; make me Christ for these people who are with me in the subway, in this car." At certain times of day, you may find yourself traveling on a line filled with immigrant workers going to or leaving their jobs. Think of them, and without staring, pray, "Lord, I offer you my own life for the life of these brothers." Other Christians of whom you are unaware may also be in the car, and among them, possibly, there is someone praying just like you. What comfort and strength we gain in knowing that we are supporting each other through a prayer that connects us.

\*    \*    \*    \*

Finally, a word on the prayer for the dead. It is a prayer full of love, mercy, and pardon. Beyond the painful absence of our loved ones, we believe that we are promised in eternal life a greater mutual presence, filled with the actual presence of God. There our pathetic bodies, inevitably disfigured by age, illness, and death, are destined to participate in the plenitude of the children of God and to share the glory of the Resurrected. To pray for the dead is to continue to live that mystical solidarity of the Body of Christ. It is to implore the mercy of God for all our brothers "who rest in Christ," just as they do for us in the unique sacrifice of Christ. It is for them as for us to await with patience "our blessed hope, the appearing of the glory of our great God and Savior Jesus Christ" (Titus 2:13), and to surmount the sadness of inescapable separations through faith that already we have received the seeds of Resurrection in our bodies.

# ELEVENTH STEP

*Sunday (1):*
*The Lord's Day*

Pray throughout the day? Well and good. But all the days of the week are not the same! Very well, then, why not begin with Sunday, which is rich not only in tradition but in meaning as well. Some of you may have forgotten that fact, or perhaps you never knew it.

First of all, a practical remark: Sunday is different from other days of the week because it is a day, if not of rest, at least of a break from the regular occupations of the week. Its specifically Christian religious character as a day consecrated to the God of Jesus Christ, our Lord, is in the process of disappearing. It is being snatched up and thrown aside by the collective rhythms of life in a city like Paris. Some people associate Sunday with mammoth traffic congestions as they return to the city from the country; for others, it is a day to stay at home, to tend to one's affairs or pursue some spare-time activity—if spare time exists.

In short, for many Sunday is nothing more than a welcome suspension of daily activities, a weekly rest. But it is the fundamental feature of the Christian faith! It derives all of its meaning from the Resurrection of Christ and the gathering of the People of God for the Eucharist. In urban society, in particular, Sunday—as experienced through radio, television, movies, open shops, and numerous possibilities for distraction—no longer has a religious stamp. For this reason, it is crucial that Christians today set themselves to accomplishing a task which is exactly the inverse of the one accomplished by the first generations of Christians.

Long ago, by the sheer force of conviction, and often at the price of martyrdom, Christians introduced into a pagan world their day of meeting for the celebration of the Eucharist in all of its brilliant import.

Thus, on February 12, A.D. 304 at Abitena, in present-day Tunisia, where Christianity was forbidden, thirty-one men and eighteen women were arrested for unlawful assembly on a Sunday. They were led by officers of the law before the proconsul, who reproached them for disobeying the imperial decree prohibiting meetings of their kind on an ordinary day, a working day. A priest, Saturninus, responded, "We have to celebrate the Lord's Day; it is our law" (even though opposed to the law of the Emperor). Emeritus, a reader in the Church, declared in turn, "Yes, it was in my house that we celebrated the Lord's Day." Finally, Victoria, a young woman consecrated to God, professed, "I went to the meeting because I am a Christian."

All forty-nine were martyred for having been faithful to a commandment which has since become a commandment of the Church: to mark their adherence to Jesus Christ, Christians are to observe Sunday by taking part in the Eucharistic assembly. At a time when all days were working days, it was Christians who forged Sunday into a day of rest.

\* \* \* \*

Contemporary society lives through Sunday after Sunday without even thinking about its remarkable origin. That is why we members of the body of Christ must do the opposite of what was done formerly: we must restore a Christian meaning to a day of rest; whereas formerly, it was the Christian meaning that transformed a working day into a day of rest.

Rendering its Christian sense to Sunday means that we must refuse to let ourselves be swept along in the current of what everybody else is doing—just as with everything in our lives. O my friends! I address myself to all of you, my brothers and sisters in the faith who live your Christian existence as best you can, sometimes very much alone. Whether you are a child or adolescent, recently married or a grandparent, whether you live alone or in a family, you must rediscover the significance of this weekly event which marks our lives. You must reinvent, by the sweat of your brow, the Christian meaning of this day. It must be made into a day of faith and joy.

The true dimension of Sunday is not immediately evident. Although it plays a decisive role in Christian life, which brought it into being, it may appear to have been given to us by the customs and habits of our society. Absolutely not! Society does nothing more than to provide us with a free day; it is up to Christians to reinvest that day with its full religious import. The task rests entirely with us. In accomplishing it we shall be tightening the bonds of the Christian community; and in our social as well as personal life, we shall be giving body and face to our faith in Jesus Christ.

\*   \*   \*   \*

The means and opportunities are multiple. Of course, a foundational place must be accorded to the

Eucharist, to prayer, and to pardon. Put on your Sunday best! Getting dressed in our "Sunday best," as we used to say, alludes not so much to dressing ourselves in finery as to dressing our hearts and souls in the clothes of the Resurrection.

We have to transform the elementary gestures of ordinary life into celebrations that restore Sunday's sacred sense. It is a time to experience the blessing of a meal shared in fraternal joy, to give special attention to family relations which may need rekindling after the ups and downs and distortions of daily life. Finally, we have to revive the traditional customs of inviting or visiting the poor, the foreigner, the isolated, and the ill.

In a word, the authenticity of the experience of the "eternal" in each Sunday firmly anchors Christians in that original and fundamental event which has made us what we are: Christ is risen, and he comes to live in the midst of us, his people gathered in his name.

\*　\*　\*　\*

Here is what the *Constitution on the Sacred Liturgy* (106), the first text voted by the Fathers of the Council of Vatican II on December 4, 1963, has to say on the subject of Sunday. The gist of what we have to discover is summed up here:

"By an apostolic tradition which took its origin from the very day of Christ's resurrection, the Church celebrates the paschal mystery every eighth day; with good reason this, then, bears the name of the Lord's Day or the Day of the Lord. For on this day Christ's faithful should come together into one place so that, by hearing the word of God and taking part in the Eucharist, they may call to mind the passion, the resurrection and the glorification of the Lord Jesus, and may thank God who 'has begotten us again, through the resurrection of Jesus Christ from the dead, unto a living hope' (1 Peter 1:3). Hence, the Lord's Day is the original feast day, and it should be proposed to the piety of the faithful and taught to them in such a way that it may become in fact a day of joy and of freedom from work."[1]

You have noted that the Council refers to Sunday as the eighth day. All four Gospels underline the fact that Christ, resurrected on "the first day of the week," appeared on that same day to Mary Magdalene and Mary, to Peter, to the two disciples on their way to Emmaus, and to the assembled Apostles when only Thomas was missing (cf. Matthew 28:1; Mark 16:9; Luke 24:1; John 20:1). The day that will become the first Sunday falls on "the first day," "eight days later," as Saint John (20:26–29) points out. He continues, ". . . His disciples were again in the house, and Thomas with them. The doors were shut, but Jesus came and stood among them, and said, 'Peace be with you.' . . ."

\* \* \* \*

The naming of the days of the week by counting them (the first, the second, the third . . .) was adopted first by the Jews and later by Christians as a way of radically disassociating themselves from the astral cults of the pagans, who placed their days under the signs of their gods. Thus, Sunday was the day of the sun, Monday the day of the moon, and so forth. This profane usage has been retained in French (except for

---

[1] *The Documents of Vatican II;* Walter J. Abbott, S.J., General Editor, The America Press, 1966.

*dimanche,* precisely, which comes from *dies dominica,* the day of the Lord), and often in the Germanic and Anglo-Saxon languages.

The Latin Christian liturgy, however, was based on the Hebrew manner of designating the days. *Feria secunda* (the second day), Monday; *feria tertia* (the third day), Tuesday, and so forth.

On the sixth day, our Friday, Christ was crucified; and on the seventh day, our Saturday—the Sabbath—the buried Christ entered into the joy of God. On the eighth day (or the first day of the week), he was resurrected.

Sunday is, therefore, the Lord's Day, the day we celebrate the accomplished Resurrection of Christ and affirm our hope in his glorious Second Coming.

# TWELFTH STEP

## Sunday (2): First Day of the New Creation

Sunday is the day of the Lord (and the Lord is Jesus Christ). It was celebrated and shaped by the first Christians. Then, in A.D. 321, the Emperor Constantine made it a holiday. Thus, for sixteen centuries social life in the Christian world has been structured around a typical creation of the Christian experience. As I said in the last step, our Fathers in the faith, very early on, referred to Sunday as the "eighth day."

But a week has only seven days. How and why did the designation the *eighth day* come about? The superimposement of the eighth day on the first day of the beginning week was intended to emphasize the fact that Sunday was not simply the sabbatical day of rest transferred to a succeeding day, that it was not a substitution for the Sabbath, and that it did not invalidate the historical significance of the Jewish Sabbath in God's plan for the salvation of mankind.

\* \* \* \*

When we read the first biblical account of the Creation, which took place in seven days, we might be tempted to transpose to Sunday all that is said there about the seventh day, from which the Sabbath originated. But the first generations of Christians were well aware that they were not dealing with the same reality, and that it was not optional, *a fortiori* innocent, to take over the facts of "sacred history" and apply them to a purpose other than that determined by God.

What, then, is the import of the seventh day as it is presented to us in the first chapter of Genesis? The cycle of seven days expresses a particular vision of the world. In the first days, God reveals himself as the Creator, sovereign Goodness, and sovereign Master of all Creation in which he manifests himself. God, who has created all things, sees that they are good; that is, that they reflect his own goodness. At the culmination of Creation, on the sixth day, God creates man so that he can share in his divine life. Thus, the "vacation" which falls on the seventh day is neither an admission of fatigue nor of the worker's need for rest after a week of labor. It is much more! It is the epiphany—the "making clear"—of God's completion of Creation and his purpose for man: union with him, the Creator.

After the progressive unfolding of the universe, after man has been brought forth from the creative Breath, God, on the seventh day, gathers him into his own plenitude and his own peace. The observance of the seventh day as a day of rest is not the mere execution of an order coming from on high: "My friends, you have worked hard for six days; now you must rest. It is a sacred day and you are not to engage in any utilitarian work." No. The significance of the seventh day stems from the very purpose for which we were created. Men, created in the image and likeness of God—Children of God, created free and made masters of Creation—the purpose of your life is not to possess the world entrusted to you only as a means; it is to live with God and from God. The purpose of all that we do on earth is to enter finally into the peace of God. This is the sense of the seventh day: it is the culmination of Creation when the Creator in love draws his creature to him.

* * * *

The eighth day—the day of the resurrected Christ, present with his assembled people—connotes that the world, brought forth from the hands of the Creator and entrusted to man at the same time as his freedom, is a world henceforth redeemed and delivered. Within the first Creation, a new Creation is already being prepared, as Isaiah prophesied (65:17): "For behold, I create new heavens and a new earth; and the former things shall not be remembered . . ."

God, our Redeemer, creates a new world whose splendor outshines that of the first Creation because he saves his creature by the Messiah and sends him the gift of the Holy Spirit. From that moment, the Christian Sunday attests to and proclaims that our present world, so cruelly disfigured by sin, is already, through hope, being transfigured. Its completion, awaited like a gift at the end of human history, is made present to us beginning now. The eighth day mysteriously inaugurates the time to come, the "already here" and the "not yet," the time of the perfection of the new Creation restored in Christ.

Sunday is fundamentally the day of the Lord. Christ, Savior of men, is wrested from death and resurrected. More than an anniversary, it is a past event always present; an event in which, by the gift of the Spirit, we take part. It is the actual occurrence of the Passover of Christ. Furthermore, it is the day when, by an act of hope, we anticipate the glorious Second Coming of the resurrected Lord, now hidden from our eyes and seated at the right hand of the Father. On Sunday, we express our faith that he will come to culminate the history of the world and of humanity with the Resurrection of the dead and the Judgment.

Each Sunday the Church announces, not the end of the world, but its perfection, which we are presently unable to grasp. Each Sunday is a cry of hope: our existing world with its face of sadness and mourning will disappear. Already we dress ourselves in wedding garments, already we see the breaking dawn and catch a glimpse of the grandeur of the Children of God. With our eyes turned toward that "anticipated" vision of happiness destined for all, we Christians become the prophets of a Sun which is rising. However, because of the obscurity in our world, groaning with birth pangs, the light of that Sun shines only in the hearts of believers who love God and put their hope in him, the disciples of Jesus, light of the world (cf. Luke 1:78 and 2:32; John 8:12; Matthew 5:14).

God convokes us to the Sunday Eucharist in order to bind us into a people and to give us strength through communion in the paschal sacrifice. He assembles us as his Church, where we experience the joy of finding ourselves again among brothers, and he shapes us, truly, into the body of his Son by sharing his Word with us, and by nourishing us with his Body and Blood, given up for us.

The celebration of the Eucharist is at the very heart of every Sunday. It is the principal event which unites the Church. By participating in the Sunday Mass, Christians inscribe in history—with a hope that is obstinate, unflagging, and indestructible—the apostolic mission which is uniquely theirs. And that is why the Sunday Mass is of primordial importance. Whether to go or not is not a decision to be based on the individual's notion of convenience, as when a person says, "I prefer to jog on Wednesday mornings because the children sleep late then," or "I always swim on such a day rather than another because the pool is less crowded then."

\*   \*   \*   \*

As God's people, we bear the collective responsibility for the history of the world; and the coming together for the Sunday Eucharist has an incommensurable importance. It is not a private or individual obligation. It is above all an unequivocal duty for all the Church, which proclaims in this way that the world is redeemed and that the time of salvation is being brought nearer by the faith and hope that live in the hearts of its members. The Church is the sign of the new Creation which is being inscribed in the old one. It is brilliant with the joy of Redemption and deliverance in a world marked by servitude, the joy of the freedom enjoyed by God's children in a world that is prisoner of itself, the joy of love and pardon in a world riddled—alas—with hate and violence, the joy of life in a world marked by death.

Much more than a duty for the individual Christian, the Sunday Mass is a mission for all the Church, which must celebrate the Lord's Day. Some of you will remember how for so many decades we heard quite bitter comments on the hypocrisy of practicing Christians, on the way people went to Mass as a mere formality or because of a need to show off, or because they worried about "what people would say" if they did not go. The page has been turned. The world has changed.

Nobody today goes to Mass to be seen or to show off fine clothes! We go to live and to recall the true significance of Sunday: *"Christ is risen!"* And he is there at the Eucharist to meet his people who have gathered together in his name.

# THIRTEENTH STEP

## Sunday (3):
## The Church's Day

So long as human history lasts, the celebration of the Mass on Sunday, the day of the Lord's Resurrection, is the first and foremost duty of the Church in its earthly pilgrimage. This duty is entrusted to the Church as a treasure and admission. I remind you of this because in our times we are not familiar enough with this perspective.

It is actually on Sunday—when it assembles with the bishop and the priests who share his sacramental ministry and have been given to the Church so that it can celebrate the Eucharist with all the people of God —that the Church takes its form, proclaiming the presence of Christ—Head and Body—in the history of men. And every Christian is duty bound to participate personally in the eucharistic sacrifice of Christ, which the Church *must* celebrate. The reverse is not true, as we might be tempted to think in this individualistic and consumer-oriented age.

We frequently hear the complaint, "Why should I have to go to Mass on Sunday if I don't feel like going? Why must I go on Sunday if I prefer to go on Wednesday?" If you think that you, all by yourself, are the Catholic Church and the measure of what God asks of his Church, very well, then, go ahead and, all by yourself, make the Church you want!

I repeat, however: the primary reason for the celebration of the Sunday Eucharist is not so that each baptized person can fulfill an individual obligation. Do you regard the Church as a kind of "distributor" of Masses, making them available to everyone so that he can do what he wants, when he wants? The Sunday Mass is not a "service" which every Christian should find within easy reach, like telephone booths, newspaper stands, and automatic banking.

The Church satisfies neither its own desires nor those of its members. It responds to an indispensable mission received from God through his Son. The Church is the face of Christ-Servant in the world, and at the same time, it is the sign of the joy of the Resurrected. Since the Church must celebrate the Eucharist on Sunday, the presence of each member is essential. If he really feels that he belongs to Christ, then each Christian fulfills the duty—an imperative duty—or participating in the very mission of the Church, which is to inscribe the witness to the Resurrection of our Lord and Master in human history. Therefore, the Sunday Eucharist celebrated by the Church is a necessity for each Christian.

We should not, however, go there like beaten dogs: "Oh, it's Sunday again, and I have to go to Mass. What a chore!" If it is like that for you, ask God to convert you, and to lift the cloud of bitterness that hangs over your heart. Ask him to let you discover the joy, grace, and generous gift which you, called now to take part in the Church's mission in the world, received at your baptism.

Yes, go to Sunday Mass at all costs. There are other reasons for going—reasons stemming from love—

which give the strength to so many Christians throughout the world, today as in the past, to risk their lives and
freedom in order to meet for the Sunday Eucharist.
The witness of these brothers and sisters should force us
to take stock of our own "lukewarmness." (If that image
strikes you as belonging to a traditional language of
pious exhortation, then go and read the "Letter to the
Church at Laodicea" in Revelation 3:14–22).

Admittedly, there do exist circumstances that
make going to Sunday Mass unfeasible. In thinking
about the situation in Paris, I can point to three.

To begin with, there is the physical impossibility of
going for those who are ill or immobilized, whether by
infirmity or age. If you belong to this group, you should,
by prayer and the communion of saints, join yourself
with all your heart, desire, and soul to your fellow Christians who are meeting in your parish church. Choose a
specific hour (no visitors) and space (a "prayer corner"
in your room, perhaps), and help yourself, when you
can, with a radio or television Mass. Remember that the
Christians in your parish have an obligation to pray for
you and for all the other members of the parish who are
absent or suffering. They also have the obligation to
bring the Eucharist to those who desire it.

You who are ill, alone and without a family—I, your
bishop, entreat you in the name of Christ—do not hesitate to get in touch with the closest parish church.
Write a note, telephone, explain who you are, why you
are unable to attend Mass on Sunday, and ask that communion be brought to you, preferably on Sunday. I
assure you that the Christian communities will arrange
to respond to your request. A priest will come if he can;
if not, then a nun or layman who has received the

mission.[1] The Church as an obligation to come to you and, thus, to associate you with the eucharistic assembly. In all likelihood, you have in the past attended Mass at the church in your neighborhood. Join the congregation again through your thoughts and your prayers. May you be able to thank God for the joy he gives you in allowing you to receive the body of Christ along with your fellow Christians, and may you be able to offer yourself with them in Christ for the "praise and glory of his name, for our good, and the good of all the Church."

Another case that comes to mind—more difficult, perhaps, and more frequent than you might think—is the moral impossibility of going to Sunday Mass. For example, some people live in families or environments so hostile to the faith that either it cannot be made known or, if it is, it is not respected. Such circumstances raise perplexing and delicate questions which touch the sensibilities and mutual love of close relations.

If in order to prevent great discord or offense to others, you are obliged to remain silent or discreet about belonging to Christ, and if, in particular, you cannot show your adherence on the Lord's Day, then, in secret, let your fervent prayer rise up to God: *My God, today is Sunday and I must make the sacrifice of abstaining from the Eucharist and the visible communion of your assembled Church. Give me, O my God, I beg of you, all the spiritual gifts which you want me to*

---

[1] Conforming to the norms regarding the worship of the eucharistic mystery: "Instructions of the S.C. for the sacraments and divine worship," 17 April 1980. And also *"Immensae Garitatis* instruction for facilitating the possibilities of access to the sacramental communion in certain circumstances," 29 June 1973.

*have, all which you have destined for me; and give to those with whom I live, and because of whom I am staying at home rather than going to Mass, the signs of your love. Grant that one day they will know you, recognize you, and accept you who are the true and living God.*" In this way, you can transform your privation of the Eucharist into a participation in the eucharistic sacrifice. The Church teaches that the faithful who find it impossible to commune share, by their "spiritual communion," the same grace of the love of Christ as those who are present. With discretion, find a time to read the scriptural passages for the day, and pray, even if only briefly, one of the eucharistic prayers.

During the week, arrange a way of going to Mass, not that it will replace the Sunday celebration, but so as not to deprive yourself further of that unique nourishment, indispensable for Christians: the Eucharist, the gift of Christ, without whom we would be nothing.

Finally, there are still other Christians (merchants, civil servants, the personnel of public services, hospitals, etc.) whose work schedules deter them from taking part in the Sunday Eucharist.

To all I dare to say, "Don't give up so easily!" Look closely at a listing of Masses available to you. There are plenty of evening Masses on both Saturday and Sunday. If necessary, when there are several of you in the same situation (employees at a railroad station, for example), go and present your case to a priest in the parish nearest to the station, and he can, if need be, discuss the problem with a priest in the adjacent parish. Not one of the faithful—priest or layman—should cede to a practical obstacle before having tried to do everything possible to overcome it. I am certain that neither imagination nor flair for initiative is lacking among you.

\* \* \* \*

Can a person choose where he goes to celebrate the Eucharist? That is not an easy question, but in our times it has to be raised. I know, it all depends! Besides the practical considerations (distances, transportation, weekend plans, etc.), the location of one's residence has to be taken into account. Territorial limits, often arbitrary, specify the extent of each parish. But the fact of "living on such and such a street, which falls within the boundaries of such and such a parish" is not sufficient to give a person the overriding sentiment of belonging to that parish. All the more so since the great majority of Christians does not even know where parish boundaries lie. Living in a large city has accustomed us to a considerable mobility. For example—I am speaking now as a former parish priest—certain people attend a church because it is more convenient to get to it by taking a direct bus or subway line than to walk to the nearest parish church. Many people are even unaware of the way to reach the church nearest them or, indeed, unaware of its very existence, not having spotted it because of its concealment by surrounding buildings.

Attending Mass in a particular parish is subject neither to imperative law nor to administrative norms. Our connection with the Christian community is also a function of the urban realities that we experience. Without going so far as "shopping around" for a church, it is important to take into account the diverse factors over which city planners are beginning to have better control.

There are other factors, however, that we also have a right to consider: our tastes and sensibilities, with their more or less well founded reactions. Thus people will say, "We are in a big city with many churches. I feel comfortable in a certain community; in another, not at all. I feel spiritually nourished in a certain parish congregation; in another, not at all." Assuredly, the problem is complicated.

\* \* \* \*

Above all, however, there are two principles to keep in mind when making your decision:

• First, we must accept with realistic love the Church as it is in any specific parish. We did not choose it. (The hazard of our address "assigned" us to it.) It did not choose us. (Had you thought about turning the question around?) This double admission, as it turns out, is a *practical* illustration of a fundamental characteristic of the Church and the love that unites its members. Jesus says to his Apostles, "It is not you who have chosen me; it is I who have chosen you." Similarly, members of the Church have not chosen one another. We have been chosen and brought together by Christ in spite of our differences, indeed, in spite of our incompatibilities. It is Christ and his love that bind us together. He gives us to each other to love *as* he loves us.

Certainly, the Church as it is can make us suffer. (The celebrant displeases us; so does the congregation; the liturgy does not suit us. . . .) Such reactions are normal. What do you expect? Charity is always crucifying! If we love only those who love us, or those whom we think we love, that means that we turn inward and never come out of ourselves. Sartre said, "Hell is others." I would readily retort, "Paradise is others, but at the cost of bearing the Cross." The person who pleases us completely and is no different from us is not really "other," but a reflection of ourselves. We do not see him as he is, but the way we dream him to be. For the sinful and wounded humans that we are, "others" are always a source of suffering without which there is no joy in loving or being loved. So accept the Church as it is.

• The second point is that we must assure our spiritual revival through the Sunday Eucharist. The depth of that revival can be measured neither by the desire we have for the Eucharist nor by what we feel, but only by the fruits of faith, hope, and charity which subsequently bear.

For the coming week, then, my Christian brothers and sisters, I wish you a "Happy Sunday." May the joy of the resurrected Christ, the joy of God's people assembled in his Church be with you all, whether you are alone or with your family, whether personally present or participating in private. I shall pray for all of you.

# FOURTEENTH STEP

*Sunday (4):*
*How to Profit*
*from the Mass*

The Sunday Eucharist is both the base and summit of the life of the Church, just as prayer and holiness are for the life of the individual Christian. When we take part in the Mass, we reunite ourselves with the Church wherever it is gathering and we accept it as it is given to us, not as we dream it should be. We do not choose our fellow Church members the way we choose friends and acquaintances. A person can no more select his brothers in the faith than he can select his parents, siblings, or children. Spiritual progress consists in our discovering those Church brothers unchosen by us and recognizing that they, chosen and loved by God, are a source of sanctification and love for us because they communicate the love which comes from God, which is God. We must love them, even though the association of those two words—must and love—appears to be contradictory.

Admittedly, feeling spiritually revived after Sunday Mass can imply that I have communed in a place where I am at ease, where I am aided in prayer, where I enter into a better understanding of the mystery of God and, thus, nurture my faith. However, as soon as I have grasped the nature of a true relation to the Father and the Son in the Spirit, and the nature of charity, hope, and the reality of the Church in its unique richness, then, gradually, I will become capable of accepting the Church as it is, even if it makes me suffer. Sinner that I am, I, too, wound the body of Christ and disfigure his face.

The more we discover the faithfulness of God and the abundance of his love, the more he gives us the strength to think less about ourselves and more about accepting others, even to the extent of rejoicing that they are there and that we are fraternally assembled by the grace of God. Having said that, I realize that we have to take into account what we are, our stages of spiritual growth, and what God has given us to live. If you are constantly ill at ease in a particular church, in a particular parish or community, then there is no point in forcing yourself beyond your limits. Start to think about how and where you can fruitfully participate in the Sunday Mass. Meanwhile, pray that God will pardon your weaknesses. Instead of blaming others, blame yourself for not being able to accept your brothers as they are. Once you have admitted your failure with humility—which is more realistic and honest than remaining in a situation where you are repeatedly being rubbed the wrong way or finding yourself rowing against the current—God will give you the grace, little by little, to step forward to meet those who are different. And eventually, when God wishes it, you will be able to welcome them with joy.

\* \* \* \*

What is the best way to profit, if I may use that word, from the Sunday Eucharist? As a first step, I strongly urge you to take your Bible or missal and read beforehand the parts of the Holy Scriptures that will be contained in the Liturgy of the Word.[1] It will take you no more than ten minutes; it is not forbidden, however, to spend more time at it, by adding readings from the previous or following Sundays, for example. You will hear the texts all the more clearly, and your understanding will be all the deeper for having read and meditated on them. From one Sunday to another you can also put the "continuous" Gospel readings in their contexts by filling in the inevitable gaps. I suggest that you follow the liturgical calendar and read one of the three synoptic Gospels (Matthew, Mark, Luke) in its entirety. You can add, along with the Church, the Gospel of Saint John. This evangelistic itinerary spread out over the course of the liturgical year (Advent, Christmas, etc.) leads us along the same road traveled by Jesus, making it possible for us to follow more attentively the mystery of his life.

*  *  *  *

Prepare the readings from the Word of God, and sometime, also, the Eucharistic Prayer itself, which the priest pronounces aloud. As you know, four principal forms of the prayer are proposed in the liturgy of the Church. They are known as Prayers I, II, III, and IV. The first is the most venerable because it dates back to the beginnings of Christianity. A prayer of the Church of Rome (hence, the name "The Roman Canon"), it originated in the Orient. The three other prayers are

---

[1] References to the weekday and Sunday readings can be found in various liturgical calendars, published each year, including some small ones which easily slip into your Bible.

based on ancient texts and were recomposed after the Council of Vatican II.

Make the effort to peruse and meditate, word for word, each of the four eucharistic prayers. From the infinite riches you will find there, you will be able to derive a framework for personal prayer and contemplation. On Sunday, when the priest speaks these words, your prayer will be immeasurably nourished because they will have become a part of you. The phrases that the priest proclaims are of such density that it is impossible to perceive all their meaning in the brief time it takes to speak them. Moreover, their density increases the risk that you will simply not pay attention and think, "What are those words trying to say? I've lost the train of thought. I don't understand." Of course, you do not understand because you have never taken the trouble to try to understand, or taken the time to reflect on the inexhaustible mystery that they convey. The pages whose meaning we perceive with increasing acuity are not those we have read once, "understood" once, and put aside once and for all with resignation: "I've already heard it, I've already read it, I'm not going to linger over it any longer." On the contrary, it is only by meditating a text frequently and at length that we can discover its greatest treasures. That is true *a fortiori* of the Word of God and the liturgical texts of the Church.

\* \* \* \*

Finally, several days before the Sunday Mass, set aside a time to reflect on its meaning, about the renewed joy you have Sunday after Sunday in being plunged into the mystery of the Resurrection of the Lord, who is always present in his Church. Anticipate the weekly rendezvous that Christ makes with his Church—just as friends and engaged couples arrange to see each other regularly—and you can exclaim, "My God, what a joy it will be to see you again! What a pleasure it will be to meet for such a celebration, such an event!" Sometimes it is good for us to live a little in expectation, tasting and savoring in advance what is to come.

Certainly that statement applies to the Sunday Eucharist. Rejoice in the thought that in a few days you will be able to join the ecclesiastical assembly which welcomes the coming of Christ into its midst; the assembly which permits you to receive the gift of Christ himself, in his Body and his Blood; the community which offers you the grace to live as a brother among brothers in the faith of the Church. And then, in anticipation of the Sunday Mass, faithfully weave the threads of your preparation into the remaining days of the week.

\* \* \* \*

When Sunday comes, try to avoid arriving at the church at the last minute. Silence your hypercritical tendencies, and leave your inclination to irritability at the door. Drop your defensive attitude, and decide to do what is asked of you: take a songbook, walk all the way down the aisle to the front rows, or what have you. With a spirit of goodwill, make a special effort to adapt yourself to the celebration as it is presented. Even if you are feeling worn down by fatigue, cares, and prejudices, keep repeating to yourself that at this Mass when Christians are coming together, many marvels are being offered to you by the benevolence of God himself.

If you are a person who can easily become enthusiastic about a liturgy which suits you, one which allows you to find joy and nourishment, so much the better! But if you have a despondent, fault-finding temperament, beware! You must not allow your spiritual revival to be impeded by the deficiencies of the celebration, whatever they may be (a church that is aesthetically displeasing, a poorly prepared liturgy, an awkward priest, an "out-of-place" sermon, annoying laymen, poor singing, etc.). You can still profit from all that is being given to you because *"in everything God works for good with those who love him"* (Romans 8:28). In the midst of all that may be upsetting you, God is waiting with a message he wants you to understand. If you arrive at the church with your fists clenched, your heart sullen, your eyes closed, and your ears plugged, you will not be able to receive that message. Never forget for an instant that through the priest who is speaking—without his knowing how, without your knowing how—God wants to reveal himself.

\* \* \* \*

What hope, what grace has God intended for you at this Mass? That is the *only* question that you must loyally ask yourself. With the same charity that God shows for each person, you can compensate for the inadequacies that bother you. How? By an attitude of openness to God and to brotherly love. Volunteer, if you can, to help in some parish activities: but guard against acting as though you have a thing or two to teach everybody else involved. Live more charitably, with more understanding, more attention to others, more hope, more prayer, more worship, more joy.

In every Sunday Mass, God makes himself known, he sacrifices himself, he brings us together to commune in his holiness through his Son Jesus, in the Spirit who sanctifies the Church.

# FIFTEENTH STEP

*Throughout the Year:*
*The Time of Salvation*

The liturgical cycle, which designates certain periods of the year according to an itinerary proposed by the Church, leads Christians into the mystery of Christ by following from Sunday to Sunday the path of a synoptic Gospel: Year A, Saint Matthew; Year B, Saint Mark; Year C, Saint Luke. The beginning of the Christian year, then, is not the first day of January, but the first Sunday of Advent. Time is marked in depth not by the earth's revolution around the sun, but by the events in the history of our salvation in Jesus Christ: the anticipation of the Messiah, his coming at Christmas and Epiphany, his baptism and temptations in the desert, his public life, his ascent toward Jerusalem (our period of Lent), Easter, Ascension, Pentecost. . . .

The Church proclaims this progressive "time of salvation" by its liturgical calendar, which inscribes in our time the times of the Savior, from the first Sunday of Advent to the Sunday of Christ the King.

\* \* \* \*

In social and private life, time passes within an entirely different framework, at an entirely different pace, which the Church today does not have the means to restructure. (Remember what I said about the origin of Sunday as a holiday). The year goes by punctuated by secular holidays as well as by holidays that are Christian in origin (Christmas, Easter, etc.), but which are losing more and more of their religious significance. For many of our contemporaries, they mean nothing more than a welcome break from work or school. On a personal level, a year is marked by other important occasions. Within the month or the year, some people will be facing crucial academic examinations, military service with its scheduled leaves and maneuvers, the beginning of a professional life, a change of jobs, retirement, matrimony, or the birth of a child.

In the coming year, then, with its more or less predictable events as well as its unexpected ones in our individual and collective lives, the Church proposes another way of dividing time, with Christ as the only reference. Hidden in the glory of the Father, he is present and at work in human history, as he promised us: "And, lo, I am with you always, to the close of the age" (Matthew 28:20).

\*    \*    \*    \*

Within the perspective of our faith, we are invited to perceive and live the reality of the time of salvation, which continues in the mission entrusted to the Church. We are to be witnesses to it by living with the same fervor and faith as the Virgin Mary, who "kept all these things in her heart" (Luke 2:19, 51). In sharing the life of Christ of Nazareth (his "hidden life" we call it because it was the life of an ordinary person covered in obscurity), Mary was able to see the fulfillment of the hope of salvation. Later, in the public life of her Son, she observed with the keenly perceptive eyes of a mother the unfolding of the plan of Redemption, as yet incomprehensible to those who were to be its first beneficiaries. The time came, not so long afterward, when they, too, were overjoyed by the gift of the Spirit, who not only inspired them with the knowledge of God, but also with the courage that comes from faith in him. Then, the Apostles of Jesus, in their turn, became the signs and artisans of the promised salvation.

In non-Christian countries (on the continent of Asia, for example), or in a civilization that is losing sight of the specific character of Catholic religious holidays and in which, as a result, society no longer has any explicit Christian reference, it is imperative that the disciples of Christ be present at all times to their Lord and Master, who remains present to us throughout our lives. In the weeks and months ahead, we Christians must become living witnesses to the salvation accomplished by Christ, thus fulfilling one aspect of our sacerdotal and mediatory role in an increasingly secularized world. We are to render present the reign of God in the passing history of mankind.

\*    \*    \*    \*

The importance of liturgical time to our mission is capital. It helps us to surmount the "wear and tear" of our daily life by referring us to the major event in human history. The organization and construction of our lives in the light of faith, however, requires our adoption of a fundamental attitude. The Church reminds us of it in the Gospel proclaimed each year on the first Sunday of Advent: "Watch,"[1] "Watch at all times, praying that you may have strength . . ."[2]

---

[1] Matthew 24:42 for Year A and Mark 13:35 for Year B.
[2] Luke 21:36 for Year C.

Christ, when speaking to his disciples about his Second Coming, explains it this way (cf. Mark 13:4–32): "It is like a man going on a journey, when he leaves home and puts his servants in charge, each with his work, and commands the doorkeeper to be on the watch. 'Watch therefore—for you do not know when the master of the house will come, in the evening or at midnight, or at cockcrow or in the morning—lest he come suddenly and find you asleep!' And what I say to you I say to all: Watch."

To watch is to pray. Jesus often associates the two words, notably at Gethsemane, when he asked Peter, James, and John to *"watch and pray"* with him (cf. Matthew 26:41). To watch is also to live from faith. In the middle of the night we must struggle not only to stay awake ourselves, but to keep awake those people around us who are overcome by sleep and tempted to run away. As we wait for the dawn, we must keep our eyes firmly fixed on the horizon, while keeping the light of Christ aglow within ourselves. The mission of the entire Church and of each Christian is this vigilance in faith and in prayer. No matter how humble, isolated, or ignored your life is, not matter what your age, influence, state of health—even if you are ill or without external activities because of failing strength—you are charged with this watch which is the hope of the world. You have an irreplaceable role to play in this Christian vigilance, presently concealed in our world, because the Lord has commanded it.

With the point of view opened up to us by the liturgical calendar, we can begin to plan our lives over an unimaginable length of time. What an audacious assertion! But it is true. All of us are inevitably buffeted about and thwarted in our expectations by various circumstances (illness, financial reversals, sudden changes and misfortunes of all kinds). It can seem impossible to organize our lives or to keep them "on course." But through prayer and watchfulness we anchor our faith in the mystery of the living Christ, present throughout time. I can think of him in secret; and even if the society in which I live ignores him, I can and must base my life on plans of the longest duration.

How? By inserting my life, instant after instant, into the history of the long-term plan of salvation, from the sacrifice of Abel, the Just, to the coming in glory of the Son of Man at the end of time.

\* \* \* \*

My existence can appear insignificant, my days precarious, and my occupations futile. (I attach myself to worthless things, which, in any case, I risk losing because of the uncertainties of life!) Nevertheless, I can and must plan ahead, for a very long time ahead.

*Why?* Because the objective for which each one of us is working is the salvation of the world, the Resurrection of the dead, eternal life, the Kingdom of God. *But how long does my life go on?* Beyond the end of the world. *What is the point of my life?* To live with Christ, to proclaim the goodness of God, and to live in such a way that those around you come to share your joy in knowing themselves loved by God. *How can I be certain that what I am doing is useful?* It is always useful if you do it out of love for God; in this way, you have a part in the manifestation of God's love for mankind. *But surely my suffering is in vain.* No, it is not, if you are united with Christ while you suffer. *Even so, nobody ever praises me or mentions what I have done for my family or in my work; my efforts are completely ignored; nobody even witnessed the loving gesture I made.* It was seen by your Heavenly Father, and that is sufficient. By the power of the Holy Spirit and the Communion of Saints, that gesture influences the course of history and is helping to save the world. Your life is recorded in the time of Christ, who embraces our time, the time of mankind, forevermore.

*  *  *  *

By watching and praying with a deep commitment of faith in the immeasurable span of God's plan, *"Thy Kingdom come,"* we remain truly free to live to the fullest every day that God gives us, and to place our lives in his hands at every moment. The greater our solidarity with the history of all men, the greater our freedom to commit ourselves to the Master in all aspects of our lives. With that sovereign freedom by which I wholeheartedly engage myself in the accomplishment of God's will—hence, giving my poor plans a place in the vast plan of God—I will be neither despairing nor overwhelmed, even though I may be saddened and tearful, when God says to me, *"Come now. Stop the work you are doing: I have something else in mind for you,"* or *"Here you are with virtually no strength left and your intellectual capacities seriously diminished. The circumstances of your life have been drastically altered. Maybe you are about to die."*

Would that I always be able to respond to God's gift of grace with a receptive and loving heart: *"Lord, you are going to call me back to you with love. Thy will be done,"* or *"You are asking me to do something com-*

*pletely different with my life. Thy will be done. Blessed are you, Lord, who have given me these days to live and who call me to work with you. Blessed are you, Lord, who have entrusted me with this day of my life and who permit me, in and with your Church, to share in the Redemption of humanity, because I am contributing to the history of the presence of Christ-Savior in our world."*

\*     \*     \*     \*

In shedding the light of faith on all human existence, the progression of the liturgical year by which the Church consecrates time is not only an incitement to vigilant prayer. It also allows us, day after day, to enter into a faithful and loving perspective which reveals to us the secret and true dimension of our daily lives: the plenitude of communion with God, the *Parousia.*

# SIXTEENTH STEP

*Praying to Mary*
*to Pray for Us*

As you know, every year each of the Gospel readings for the four Sundays of Advent recounts a specific time in the history of our salvation. On the first Sunday, we read a fragment of what Jesus says about the end of time. On the second and third Sundays, we are presented with John the Baptist in his mission and role as prophet and precursor of Christ. Finally, on the fourth Sunday, just before Christmas, the readings focus on the Virgin Mary: the announcement to Joseph,[1] the Annunciation,[2] and the Visitation.[3] In this way we are prepared for the celebration of the birth of Christ-Messiah, Jesus, Son of God and Son of Mary.

The place of the Virgin in the life and prayer of Christians is an indication of the equilibrium of their life and faith. Why is that so?

\* \* \* \*

First of all, a primordial remark. We do not pray to Mary in the same way that we pray to the Father, the Son, and the Spirit.

When, united with the Son because the Spirit lives within us and inspires us to pray (Romans 8:15, 16), we

---

[1] Matthew 1:18–24 for year A.

[2] Luke 1:26–28 for Year B.

[3] Luke 1:39–45 for Year C.

pray to the Father, we address ourselves to the One who is above all, beyond all, who surpasses all things. We turn ourselves toward our Father with faith, love, and hope, but at the same time as creatures before our Creator. When we beseech Christ, Jesus of Nazareth, we know very well that in his humanity he made himself our brother, but that, even so, he remains the eternal Son. When we invoke the Spirit, present in the most secret depths of ourselves, we are keenly conscious that as disciples of Christ we have been given a gift of inexpressible magnitude: thanks to the Holy Spirit, we can know and almost experience God, who, although unknowable and imperceptible, has brought himself so near that he dwells in us and we dwell in him. Nevertheless, not for a single instant do we forget that God is God and that we are his creatures.

Our way of praying to Mary is altogether different. Recite a "Hail Mary" and you will note immediately that to pray to the Mother of Jesus is *to pray to her to pray for us.* We call on someone who, like us, is a creature of God, and turns herself, just as we do, to the invisible God. Then why do we ask her to pray for us? Why not pray directly to God, who answers our prayers?

Because Mary is the Mother of Jesus. We know that from the first moments of her existence she was made holy by the benevolent grace of God. She was called and chosen by God. Her flesh was sanctified so that the Savior could become flesh in her. We know very well that Mary is totally obedient to the will of God, whose words she faithfully keeps in her heart. She is the one to whom Christ himself entrusted all his brothers, all of humanity, in the person of the beloved disciple:

"Woman, behold, your son" (John 19:26). We know all that. It is sufficient to read the Gospel with a receptive and open mind to see and understand that the Mother of the only Son of God can, as no other person, intercede to the Heavenly Father for us, her adopted sons.

\* \* \* \*

In praying to Mary to pray for us, we measure the depth of our belief in the omnipotence of prayer and we test our faith in the Church. You remember the words of Jesus, "Truly, truly, I say to you, if you ask anything of the Father, he will give it to you in my name" (John 16:23), ". . . that the Father may be glorified in the Son" (John 14:13). And again, "And whatever you ask in prayer, you will receive, if you have faith" (Matthew 21:22). Remember also, "Ask, and it will be given to you; seek, and you will find; knock, and it will be opened to you" (Matthew 7:7). And finally, there is the parable of the troublesome widow and the unjust judge that Jesus told to his disciples, ". . . to the effect that they ought always to pray and not lose heart" (Luke 18:1–8). "Vindicate me against my adversary," begs the poor woman, and the judge gives in, saying, ". . . Because this widow bothers me, I will vindicate her, or she will wear me out by her continual coming." And the Lord adds, "Hear what the unrighteous judge says. And will not God vindicate his elect, who cry to him day and night?"

With an unwavering faith in these precise words of Jesus, we clearly affirm that the prayers of the disciples of Christ—the Church—are granted when we pray to the Heavenly Father in all truth, which means lovingly submitting ourselves to his will. What God wants, we want; and what we want, God wants. That is the omnipotence of prayer. But we do not dare to believe it, because we know that our prayer is a mixture of good and bad. We are capable of asking God for something bad which stems from our caprice and not from our happiness, that is, our holiness. And we can ask God for things that appear beautiful and good to us, while the desire for those things can have arisen from our hardened hearts and darkened minds. When we are suffering and prey to misfortune, we are like wounded animals, and we no longer count on the power of prayer.

That is when, more than ever, we must pray to Mary. Mary, who is from our side, in a manner of speaking, and who shares our human condition. She represents the Church, which is already embodied in her and which she prophesies. Already in her person, the Church beseeches the Heavenly Father, implores the Son, and is submitted to the Spirit, whom it invokes. By praying to the Virgin, entrusting the answers to our prayers to her as the mediator who intercedes for us, we are not climbing an extra rung on a ladder between God and ourselves. Rather we are recognizing, in the weakness of our faith, the all-powerful faith of the Church. The Church just as God wishes her to be, as the Bride of his Son, and just as we dare to believe she is when we look at Mary, who is the source, model, and anticipation of it. Mary, Mother of the Church, Mary in whom the Church is already foreshadowed and assembled.

We love the Virgin; we speak of her with joy and simplicity; thinking of her makes us happy. This does not imply, however, that we are merely introducing into our lives a familiar feminine figure who will ease and shorten the abysmal distance which separates us from the invisible God. Certainly, God makes himself seen in his beloved Son; he makes himself heard in his Scriptures, the Word of Life. But we must accept the fact that we cannot depict him: it is he who reveals himself to us.

To pray to the Virgin Mary to pray for us indicates that we recognize what a mystery of holiness is fulfilled through her Son who came into our world on Christmas Day. It means that we recognize that in Mary we are permitted to see and understand our own condition and mission: although we are "poor sinners," we have been created to be born to and commune in the life of God.

As Christmas approaches, why not try to discover how the characteristics of the Church—"one, holy, catholic, and apostolic"—apply to the Virgin? Such a comparison sheds an extraordinary light which leads us to understand both the mystery of Mary and the mystery of the Church.

\* \* \* \*

*One.* Initially, the mere mention of the word in regard to the Church evokes a negative image: the division of Christians. But it is followed by a positive one: the task of gathering "into one the children of God who are scattered abroad" (John 11:52). It is precisely for this work of salvation that God wants us to concentrate our energies "so that the world may believe" (John 17:21). However, the unity of redeemed humanity, as it is prophesied by the Virgin Mary, is essentially the unity that comes from her motherhood. Mary, the "daughter of Zion" (as she is called by all biblical and

Christian tradition—cf. Zechariah 2:10, etc.), and the mother of the unique Savior, the Christ, becomes the unique Mother of all. In her saintly person, where the faith and holiness of Israel reach their apogee, there is the convergence of all the past generations of the People of the Covenant and, gathered in advance, all the future generations of those who will be born to life as children of God and given to each other as brothers and sisters of the Lord Jesus. Just as Jesus, on the Cross, said when he "saw his mother, and the disciple whom he loved standing near . . . 'Woman, behold, your son!' Then he said to the disciple, 'Behold, your mother!' " (John 19:26, 27)

The true unity to which we are called is fundamentally the unity of the new Creation. The maternal figure of the Virgin, the new Eve, is the prophecy and the anticipation of that Creation. We are brothers of each other, because we are brothers of her Son, because we have become one in her Son.

*Holy.* In Mary, "full of grace" which was given to her by God from the moment of her immaculate conception (Luke 1:28), we see the absolute holiness of a human being completely seized by her Creator. She is delivered from all evil, and transfigured by the presence of God in her: she is the announcement of a new world.

The child who will become flesh within her by the power of the Spirit "will be called holy" (Luke 1:35): Jesus, the Holy One of God (cf. also Mark 1:24; John 6:69). Through him, with him, in him, we are made holy by being united with him, by sharing his condition as Son and the way he obeys his Father and accomplishes his will, by sharing his work and his love for his Father and for his human brothers, all the way to the Passion. We stand, like Mary, at the foot of the Cross. "Now I rejoice in my sufferings for your sake, and in my flesh I complete what is lacking in Christ's affliction for the sake of his body, that is, the Church," Saint Paul dares to say (Colossians 1:24).

*Catholic.* The catholicity of the Church applies to Mary not in the sense of universality, but rather in regard to her making it possible for the pagan nations to share in the inheritance of the chosen people of Israel, of the "saints in light," as Saint Paul says (Colossians 1:12; cf. also Ephesians 1:18).

When the wise men from the East went "into the house, they saw the child with Mary his mother" (Matthew 2:11). The Virgin of Nazareth gave birth to the Savior of all Nations. Through him who is born of her, all people on earth have access to the knowledge of the living and true God and are invited to the wedding feast of the Lamb, just as Mary was invited to the wedding in Cana.

*Apostolic.* One of the mysteries of the Church is that a new people of God was founded on the twelve Apostles. Mary is with them in the Upper Room in Jerusalem to receive the gift of the Spirit. Her presence there announces the maternal mission of the Church throughout history: the bringing to divine life of all men because all men are loved by God.

To pray to the Virgin, Mother of Jesus, is to have recourse through her to the all-powerful intercession of the Church which she foreshadows. Daughter of Zion who joyfully receives her Savior, she is a believer to whom God listens because she is wholly attentive to him.

We pray that Our Lady, in her steadfast faith and maternal tenderness, will intercede for us *now and at the hour of our death.*